# HIDDEN

# HIDDEN

*A Sister and Brother
in Nazi Poland*

Fay Walker *and* Leo Rosen
*with Caren S. Neile*

THE UNIVERSITY OF WISCONSIN PRESS

The University of Wisconsin Press
1930 Monroe Street
Madison, Wisconsin 53711

www.wisc.edu/wisconsinpress/

3 Henrietta Street
London WC2E 8LU, England

"Oyfn pripetshik," "Rozhinkes mit mandlen," "Reyzele," and "A brivele der mamen"
reprinted with permission from *Mir Trogn a Gezang: Favorite Yiddish Songs,* by
Eleanor Gordon Mlotek, fourth edition, copyright © 2000 by the Workmen's Circle
and Eleanor Chana Mlotek.

"Lomir zikh iberbetn" and "Belz" reprinted with permission from *Pearls of Yiddish Song,*
compiled by Eleanor Gordon Mlotek and Joseph Mlotek, copyright © 1988 by the
Education Department of the Workmen's Circle.
Maps courtesy of Tom Neile.

Library of Congress Cataloging-in-Publication Data
Walker, Fay.
Hidden: a sister and brother in Nazi Poland /
Fay Walker and Leo Rosen; with Caren S. Neile.
p.: cm
ISBN 0-299-18060-3 (cloth: alk. paper)
1.  Walker, Fay. 2.  Rosen, Leo. 3.  Jews—Poland—Kanczuga—Biography. 4.  Holocaust,
Jewish (1939–1945)—Poland—Kanczuga—Personal narratives. 5.  Kanczuga (Poland)—
Biography.  I. Rosen, Leo. II. Neile, Caren S. III. Title.
DS135.P63 A175 2002
940.53'18'09224386—dc21
2002002341

*To our beloved families and friends*

*among the living and the dead.*

*You are always in our hearts.*

The true tale of the hunt will never be told, until it is the lion who does the telling.

—*African proverb*

This memoir is the result of an intensely creative collaboration between those who experienced the events it describes and one who attempted to bring their stories and their loved ones back to life on the page. All conversations are presented according to the authors' best recollections and represent their effort to recreate what was actually said.

# Preface

Every Holocaust survivor's story is the same. In the beginning, we lived much like you, with birthday gifts and family tiffs and the occasional, inevitable experience of grief. Then, gradually, too slowly to fear, yet too quickly to ignore, pain and loss edged out the happiness, like red wine spreading on a white linen cloth. Years passed; the mark was bleached many times over. But the stain remains upon our bones.

Every Holocaust survivor's story is unique. Some of us were imprisoned; some went into hiding; some impersonated Aryans; some wandered from safe house to safe house. For some, the experience pours out freely as breath; for others, it is a silent tumor in the belly.

Every Holocaust survivor's story is true. Time may blur the edges of details, but those of us who recount our wartime experiences do so because we are compelled to exhume the memories and to honor the dead.

If you cannot believe us, it is because you cannot imagine the worst. Neither can we. But we are destined to remember it.

# HIDDEN

# Prologue
## *July 1942*

We were hidden in the countryside by the time war flooded the streets of tiny Kanczuga, until the screams and bursts of gunfire were as familiar as the cries of the peddlers hawking their wares in the *rynek*, the town's main marketplace. More than a hundred of our people were executed at point-blank range in front of the Brills' house. Then early one morning, two young SS men, ably aided by the Polish police, rounded up the hundreds of Jews who had not managed to hide themselves in time. The officers deposited them in the main square, where they stood in shocked silence, some of them still in nightclothes, shivering in the sparkling dawn.

Now the police herded their prisoners past the jeering crowd and on to the synagogue. Our people struggled to stare straight ahead, but, as they trudged the dusty streets, they found themselves peering into the faces they had known all their lives, into the flat features and pale eyes of their closest neighbors, empty and cold as death.

Kanczuga's newest synagogue was a good quarter-mile from the Jewish cemetery on the edge of town. It was not quite completed, but already it was the pride of our community, a spacious sanctuary large enough to seat several hundred. That Shabbos, every inch of the shul was filled for the first time. Yet it was eerily quiet, the low murmurs punctuated only by the occasional barking of a policeman.

Our family, apart from the two of us in hiding, filled the floor by the eastern wall. Tata's brother David sat with his wife and three of their five children, Aron, Runie, and little Golda, named after our grandmother. The other two children had been on vacation with their mother's parents and had already been captured and sent to Siberia.

Wordless and watchful, our Tata fingered a pocket of his long, black coat and stroked his beard. Beside him, Mamche, her face raw from

3

weeping, rested a delicate hand on one of my sisters' shoulders. Now and then she whispered to little Tunia, who was serious even in the best of times. The child's face, olive-skinned as a Gypsy's, glistened with tears. Pretty Senia, Aryan-blond and almost a teenager, seemed out of place in this group of frightened Jews. She scanned the wan faces, searching for friends from school.

With so many bodies huddled together, the room was close with the odor of human flesh. People slept standing, straight as sentries; others twisted into unnatural positions on the floor. At some point, rain tapped a somber staccato on the roof and windows.

A poor tradesman, reverential and cowering, broke off from the crowd to consult with Tata.

"Do you think they'll deport us instead of killing us? Maybe send us away and spare our lives, God willing?"

Our taciturn father shrugged and shook his head. "Who is to say?" he asked. "I have heard that the families who didn't come to the square to be picked up were shot in their homes. We can only wait and put our faith in God. God will provide for us. God has never forsaken us."

Like everyone else, my parents had come to the shul without packing a bag. But my best friend, Bruchcia Laufer, whose family had been temporarily spared because they were engineers still useful to the Reich, visited every day with supplies. That Friday morning, she brought two white Shabbos candles. The crowded room was hushed now, as Mamche lit the trembling flames. For a moment, her face was illuminated, as if from within. When she sang the *bracha*, her shimmering soprano could scarcely be heard, so quickly did it make its way to God.

> Baruch atah adonai, elohaynu melech ha'olam, asher kiddashanu, b'mitzvatav, v'tzivanu, l'hadlik nayr shel Shabbat.

> [Blessed art Thou, oh Lord our God, King of the Universe, who commands us to light the Sabbath candles.]

Shabbos morning arrived warm and bright, but the synagogue was musky with fear. Several men began to *daven*, and Tata joined them in prayer, swaying back and forth to the familiar chants. Mamche, as a woman forbidden to pray with the men, hummed the wailing *nigunim* under her breath, her voice sweet and smooth as her homemade jam, her pitch never wavering.

4

The men were still praying when the police ordered them to leave their families and trek the short distance up the hill to the cemetery. Mamche gripped the girls harder, her fingers digging so deeply into their flesh that they squirmed, but they did not break away. Our father, never a demonstrative man, reached for our mother's hand. The gesture was so unexpected that she met his eyes with a smile. Then the butt of an unseen rifle knocked Tata squarely between the shoulder blades, and he flinched and moved on without speaking.

They traveled a short distance in wagons. A boy named Yankele Kelstecher jumped out of his wagon and disappeared into the woods before the policemen could fire. Then the men were ordered out of the wagons. Perhaps the thought of Yankele gave the men strength as they climbed in a thin, halting line along the muddy path that wove through a cornfield. They passed a scarecrow, mocking in unfettered repose. At the crest of the hill was the tree-lined cemetery, its tombstones swathed in even rows of shrubbery. As if on command, the men paused to catch their breaths and wipe their brows. They gazed out over the crest of the hill to the patchwork of fields below. For a moment, they forgot their terror and shook their heads at the lush landscape. It could not be helped; they loved this country.

A straight-backed officer handed out shovels and told them to dig.

"Keep digging," he said. "We'll tell you when you're finished."

Most of the men were spindly and weak, with soft palms more used to the Hebrew *siddur* than to the spade.

"Dig, keep digging! Thought you could get away with something, eh? Thought you could hide from us, you filthy Jews?"

When at last they were allowed to stop, the men stood in silence beside the freshly dug earth. Their faces slick with tears and sweat, they stared at the raised rifles in astonishment. At eyes opaque as marbles, that didn't look back.

Then they saw the other eyes, those of their neighbors, the customers in their shops, the people to whom they had just last week sold a loaf of bread, who gave them a good price on chickens and eggs. The goyim stood or sat on their haunches in unruly rows alongside the policemen. Whole families, with baskets of cheese and bread and homemade wine, little ones scurrying along the fringes of the crowd, hunting down field mice. The chattering spectators were in an edgy, festive mood, the women's heads bobbing in their colorful scarves.

"Żyd!" they cried. "Jew! Out with the Jews!"

The policemen raised their rifles. One hundred hearts were broken before a single shot was fired.

When it was over, the audience applauded and cheered.

The next day, the sunlight was so fierce that the women shielded their eyes when they were led outside. They climbed through the tall grass directly to the pit, as if they had done so many times before, their children sobbing at their skirts. A fetid smell they did not recognize reached their nostrils, and they covered their faces in horror.

When the policemen loaded their rifles, Senia clutched Mamche's waist. "I don't want to die!" she cried. "The sun is shining so brightly, and I am so young, Mamche. I want to grow up in this beautiful world!"

For the first time in Senia's life, our Mamche could do nothing to help. She could not hold her any closer; she could not love her any more. One policeman who witnessed this scene was so moved that, later, he would recall Senia's words to the Kwasniaks, who had worked for us back in town.

Then a bullet shattered our little sister's face, and she collapsed at Mamche's feet, spraying blood on her new white shoes. Next Tunia dropped onto Senia, her breath a shallow purr. Even before the third shot was fired, our mother fell on them both, trying to protect what no longer was hers. Beside the gunmen, the onlookers, some of whom had tied handkerchiefs over their noses to stave off the scent, clapped and shouted their approval. A burst of laughter skimmed the crowd. Neighbors clapped each other on the back, not quite meeting each other's gaze.

My brother and I were not present at our family's murder. What we know of it we know from others. But we have lived it every day for over half a century.

# Fay

These are not my shoes. When I was Faiga Rosenbluth, pampered eldest child of Balci and Itczy, beloved sister of Luzer, Senia, and Tunia, I wore elegant, dainty pumps, with two-inch heels, a gently tapering toe box, and soft, supple uppers, creamy and smooth as a pail of fresh goat's milk. My shoes told the world that I was a young lady of twenty-one, dignified and worthy of respect, from a wealthy family, with a nice home and servants and seats by the eastern wall in the old synagogue.

But then I became Fela, sometimes convincing unsuspecting villagers with my fake Christian name and my shabby clothing that I am a peasant, more often depending on good feelings toward my family to keep me safe for a few days. Now my feet are encased in rough, heavy boots, two sizes too big, muddy and scraped and stuffed with a scrap of rug to fill up the gaps and keep me warm.

These boots originally belonged to Marysia, wife of Rewer the shoemaker. My shoes would soon grow uncomfortable, I told Rewer, and they would be a sure sign of my true identity. So now Marysia has a beautiful pair of pumps two sizes too small, and I have these horrid boots that will probably save my life.

If Bruchcia or Chajka or Runia were to see me clomping down these village roads in these big old peasant boots, they would fall down laughing. I made my dress from the lining of my coat, and the coat itself is frayed and filthy. I wear Kazia's tattered stole, and my hair, once a long, tight braid, is ragged and snarled.

The thought of Bruchcia is almost too much to bear. Like her brothers, she was smart and mechanically minded. She was a photographer, one of eight children. We spent a lot of time at our Zionist youth group and planned to move together to Palestine and raise crops and babies side by side.

Chajka was long-legged and beautiful, with thick black hair that brushed her waist. She sewed her own clothes, which were as good as any I have ever seen. Runia was so movie-star gorgeous, she turned heads wherever we went. She had seven sisters. Like Chajka, she was tall and a wonderful dressmaker.

If I were to see my dear friends now, I would not laugh. I would cry in delight at finding them whole again, their beautiful selves alive and free.

When I was Faiga Rosenbluth, I knew something about shoes. My father was a rabbi and a scholar. But he was also a prominent leather wholesaler, one of the wealthiest and most revered Jews in Kanczuga, owner of a bustling store on the Ulica Kolejova and employer of my brother Luzer and my cousin Motti, who cut uppers for the shoemakers. When business was slow, we sent out the leather to have shoes made and sold them at the market.

I never handled the heavy rolls of leather, with their bitter perfume of barnyards and sweat. But I often worked alongside my father and brother as the store watchdog, gently reminding the Swietliks or the Skoczylases or the Dudeks not to leave without first paying for their purchases. I would have preferred to have been out with my friends, of course, but it was an easy job. The farmers and shoemakers greeted me with a smile and a kind word and, when I was younger, a pat on the head or a tug on my braid. Little did I know how important their good will would turn out to be.

"Faiga" means bird in Yiddish, and happy, pampered Faiga Rosenbluth lived and worked with her family and friends in a sleepy little town, free as a bird. But Fela wanders alone and friendless on a country road under a moonless sky, living in fear, and free no more.

That is how it is with me. No family, no home. New name and old, old shoes.

# Leo

Just before I woke up today, I thought I was back in my own bed—I should be so lucky! I smelled leather, which always makes me think of home. Not until I woke up for real did I know that what I was smelling was still alive and well. It must be *bashert*—fate—that I, the leather wholesaler's son, am again living with leather. Even if this time it's still on the cow.

God willing, I'll live in this big old barn for the rest of the war. Not the whole barn, but a strip of a shelf under a sloping roof, maybe a foot high and ten feet long. If anybody'd told me that when I turned seventeen, I'd be laying in the dark all day without making a sound, I would've said they were nuts. And if anybody told me I'd let my mother say goodbye and just walk away forever, I'd've said they were lying, too.

This whole place stinks of wet hay and dust and fresh animal dung. At least the straw is soft and comfortable, and I'm not broiling from the heat. (Things could always be worse!) Before we were thrown out of our homes, we lived in town, so I never knew much about animals. In *cheder*, they told us that the horse and the cow are lower forms of life than a human, who is created in God's image. But, from where I lie, boarded up behind planks of wood, I'd give up my free will for their free movement in the wink of an eye.

How I hate being cooped up here in the summer! Sometimes my heart pounds so hard, it's about to explode. I hear the kids outdoors, just on the other side of this barn, running and singing and playing some wild game. The dog yaps away. I smell the meat on the fire and the cakes in the oven, and I want to give it all up. I want to say the heck with all this! Yeah, yeah, Mamche ordered me to stay alive, to carry on the family name. (Which is pretty funny, since I've changed my first name to Lonek, to seem more Polish.) But, at this minute, I'm like Esau, so hungry when he comes back from the hunt that he'd sell his birthright to Jacob. What do I care about life, if life is lying flat on my back twenty-two hours a day in the dark in a stinky old barn?

Hitler's going to win this war, anyway. And when he takes over the world, you don't think he's going to take over this barn, too? And even if he doesn't, who cares? What do I have left? My grandparents, dead. My parents and little sisters, dead. As for Faiga, who knows? Every Jew in the world is probably dead. I MIGHT BE THE ONLY JEW LEFT IN THE WORLD. Except maybe in America, but who knows that, either? Who knows anything anymore?

The cow just licked her baby's head, and with such happiness the little guy shivered! From here, a cow's life looks pretty good.

# Fay

Because this war took away everything from me but my memories, they have become my treasured possessions. Each day as I make my way through the countryside, or hide in someone's barn, I take out some story from my past as if from a locked chest of jewels. I hold it up to the light, see it shine, and marvel that I never valued it before. Twenty-one years of memories, all safe and in perfect condition. I am happy to share them, but I would not trade them for anything. Like the kindness of the peasants who take me in off the road, they are what keep me alive.

I was four years old when my brother was born. I remember sitting cross-legged on the floor outside the bedroom, when the midwife brushed past me and into the room. She was a heavyset, no-nonsense sort of woman, with big hands and thick, pasty skin. She smelled of soap and iodine. I still remember the thud of the door as it closed behind her hefty backside.

My grandmother was still alive at the time, and usually I went next door to sit with her if my mother was busy. With a new baby coming, however, no one had time for me. The air was so heavy with tension that I could hardly breathe. Much later, I learned that Mamche's previous baby, the one who came after me, was born dead. But that day, all I knew was that I resented the arrogant woman who had taken over our home. My belly was empty, and my throat was dry.

Then I heard my Mamche weeping. What was this? I had never heard her cry before. What was that woman doing to her behind the bedroom door? In my terror, I, too, started to cry, great hiccuping sobs of fear and misery. Someone, perhaps my father, scooped me off the floor and carried me the few steps to my grandparents' house. I don't remember what we did there. But later that night, they brought me back home to show me my tiny pink brother, nestled in my mother's arms and sucking

11

quietly. I barely noticed him. Mamche's face was a cloud, transparent and indistinct. But look; she was only sleeping. When I buried my face in her warm belly, she winced but did not turn away.

Luzer was a sickly baby, with one leg slightly thinner than the other. People whispered that he also had something wrong with his heart. Those first few years, it seemed as though every time I would try to curl up on my mother's lap, she was holding my brother. I wanted her to talk to me, or feed me, or hug me, but the baby always came first. In fact, well past the time that he was technically a baby, my brother was coddled and catered to. Mamche carried him everywhere, long after he could walk.

When I complained, which I often did, I was told that he was the *ben yahid*, the only son. That made him special, more special, it was clear, than I. And, being fragile, he required even more care.

How had this happened? Hadn't I been Mamche's best little girl?

I made my feelings clear about the new baby from the start. How stupid he was, and how he couldn't sing any songs or play my games. My family never saw my point of view. No one even seemed to notice how bad he could smell sometimes! Instead, they told me I should love my brother and not call him names.

One day when Luzer was about three, I came in from my grandparents' house in search of my mother. I found her talking to the seamstress, who was holding up dressmaking fabric. Mamche's back was to me, and I grabbed hold of her legs to say hello. She wheeled around. There was Luzer sitting contentedly in her arms, looking down at me as if from a mountaintop.

Something about the sight of him up there cooing and smiling made me furious. The moment Mamche put my brother down, I was on top of him. When they finally pulled me off, he had two pink scratches like Indian war paint running down his cheeks, and he was screaming. Mamche did not hit me, but she refused to speak to me for the rest of the day. And that was punishment enough.

12

# Leo

Not much to do around here but daydream, which was always a hobby of mine anyway. Sometimes I think, enough with the day-dreams! But what else is there to do? What I'm going to do when I get out of here—that's mostly what I think about. (I never say "if" I get out.) Be a big, important businessman. Travel. Sometimes I think about dying. But, mostly, I think about my life. And when I do, it's as if they were all sitting here with me, Mamche and Tata, my uncles and aunts, my sisters, my cousins, my friends. All singing songs and telling those old stories and jokes for about the thousandth time. I'm like a prisoner in this little barn. But, in my mind, I'm free. For the first time in my life!

The earliest thing I remember happened when I was about seven. I was sitting on a wooden bench in the Polish school with another Jewish kid. We weren't related, but, compared to the Poles and Ukrainians, we might as well've been twins. Our hair was brown, and our faces, they were all angles and shadows. Worst of all were the long locks of hair at our ears. All Jewish males had to grow these *payos*. God commanded it to remind us we were Jews—as if the goyim would ever let us forget! The rest of my hair was straight and short, but the payos were always a little curled, because I twisted them so much. I wrapped them around my fin-ger like a lucky piece of string and pushed them behind my ears when my parents weren't around. Anything not to be so different. So Jewish.

The schoolroom was dark and bare. I do not exaggerate when I say that it was the last place on earth I wanted to be. I knew I'd never become a scholar like my parents wanted. While the teacher stood up front go-ing on and on about arithmetic, the numbers flew around in my head like butterflies. Too bad I didn't have a net to reach out and catch them.

Instead, I slumped over on the desk, dreaming about my favorite topic, a bicycle. To be one of those boys who were always racing around on their two-wheelers! With a bicycle I could go anywhere and still be home for supper. With a bicycle I could outrun the bums who bothered me.

As soon as the teacher let us out for the day, kids scrambled across benches and pinched one another or grabbed at each other's books. I was still thinking about that bicycle as I wandered out the door.

Then someone reached out and gave one of my payos a sharp tug. I tried not to scream, but my muffled cry was enough for them. Everybody laughed. Then they looked at me to see what I would do. What could I do? I ran all the way home, to my mother, my father, and my houseful of Jews like me.

As soon as I pushed through the doors of our store and threw my books on the counter, I was in another world. My father looked up from the leather he was cutting and smiled. Smiling he didn't do too often, so when he did, my heart always jumped a little. I waved.

I heard him point me out to the man he was talking to. Tata said, "Just a little *pisher,* and already he's got a good head for business. When he takes over this store, he's going to turn it into an empire!"

My big sister Faiga glanced in my direction. She gave me a quick nod before turning back to talk to another girl about her age. So full of herself, my sister. We got along okay, I guess. Like cats and dogs.

Then Mamche looked up. "*Mein nachusl,*" she said. She left a customer to come over and give me a hug. "Have you been crying?"

How could I be sad when she called me her pride and joy? As soon as I saw her, I felt so good it was hard to remember what I'd been crying for.

Mamche signaled to my father that she was taking me to the house. Some of the shoemakers tousled my hair as we made our way through the store, hand in hand. I felt like I had about a million friends and that nothing could ever go wrong again.

The minute we stepped into the house behind the store, I heard Faiga's voice behind us.

"Mamche," she said, "I want to show you something!"

"Then bring it into the kitchen," Mamche said. "I'm giving Luzer a snack."

Faiga came in frowning. "Oh, can't he get it himself? What I want to show you is in the bedroom!"

"Faigale! He's a little boy. You're a big, grown girl. Can't it wait just a minute?" My sister shot me a dirty look. From the security of Mamche's side of the room, I stuck out my tongue. Ha ha!

"Don't make faces, you little scamp!" she said. When Mamche moved

14

to the oven to pull out some of her special crunchy *mandelbrot,* my sister slapped my cheek. It didn't really hurt, but I played it up big.

"She hit me!" I yelled, screaming for all I was worth.

"You baby!" Faiga said, and such a face she made! She said, "You think you're so special just because you're the ben yahid. I wish we had another brother, just so you wouldn't think you were God's gift to mankind!"

"I don't think it," I said. "I know it!"

Mamche threw down the plate of cookies so hard, it bounced on the counter. "*Kindele,* please! You are brother and sister; you should love each other!"

"I love Senia and Tunia," I said.

"Well," Faiga said, "at least that's one thing we agree on!"

Mamche clapped a hand on each of our shoulders. Me she sat down in a chair. Faiga she pushed toward the door.

"Faigale, go into the bedroom. I will be there in two seconds."

"Can I have something to take with me to eat?" she asked.

"Here, have a piece of mandelbrot."

Faiga took one, but she didn't look happy. She said, "Didn't you make some of those onion pretzels yesterday?"

"They're for Shabbos," Mamche said. "Now out!"

My sister gave me one last look that, if looks could kill, would have had me on the floor. She mouthed something I didn't understand. Then she popped the almond wedge into her mouth and left the room.

Mamche filled the plate with a few more mandelbrot and brought them to the table.

"Mamche," I whispered. "Couldn't I just have one tiny piece of pretzel?"

She tried to scowl, but she was never so good at pretending. Shaking her head, she went back into the pantry. She returned with two beautiful pretzels, smothered in candied onions.

"Now please, don't tell your sister," she said, pinching my cheek. "We've had enough fighting in here for one day."

"Thank you, Mamche," I said. I reached up to hug her.

She bent down and planted a big, juicy kiss on my head.

"Will you sing me a song, Mamche?"

She hesitated. I knew what she was thinking: Faiga was waiting. The store was busy. Tata would be watching for her. But then this would just take a minute. And I would love it so much.

She sighed, took me on her lap, smoothed my hair and started to sing:

15

Oyfn pripetshik brent a fayerl,
Un in shtub iz heys.
Un der rebe lernt kleyne kinderlekh
Dem alef-beyz.

Zet zhe, kinderlekh, gedenkt zhe, tayere,
Vos ir lernt do;
Zogt zhe nokh a mol un take nokh a mol:
Komets-alef: o!

[A flame burns in the fireplace,
The room warms up,
As the teacher drills the children
In the *alef-beyz*.

Remember, dear children,
What you are learning here.
Repeat it again and again:
*Komets-alef* is pronounced *o*.]

When you grow older,
You will understand
That this alphabet contains
The tears and the weeping of our people.

When you grow weary
And burdened with exile,
You will find comfort and strength
Within this Jewish alphabet.

Our servant, Rózia Kwasniak, appeared in the doorway. I waved at her, and she winked. But when my mother was in the room, there was really nobody else.

# Fay

Kanczuga was a tiny Polish farming community at the foot of the Carpathian Mountains, south of the Kraków–Lemberg Road and just about midway between the towns of Przemyśl and Rzeszów. The first thing you saw when you approached it from the main road was the big Catholic Church, with its enormous bell that tolled every Sunday and Christian holiday. But in fact, Kanczuga had been a Jewish shtetl for centuries, and Jews made up more than half of the population. The town seal was even a yellow star of David emblazoned in the center of a blue shield.

Our town was so isolated that we had to take two trains just to get to the nearest city. To the residents of the dozens of peasant villages that surrounded it, however, Kanczuga was a bustling metropolis, a place of shops and schools and farmers' markets, of meeting neighbors and exchanging gossip, and of doing business with the Jews, whether they liked it or not.

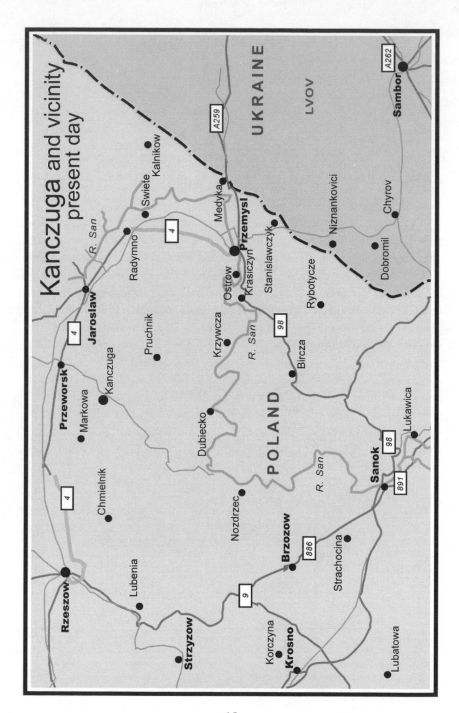

Kanczuga and vicinity present day

# Leo

Our leather shop was on the main street, Ulica Kolejova. The basement we rented out to a butcher. Next door was a tobacco seller, and a candy store next to that.

Because our house was attached to the store, it doubled as our storeroom. Leather was everywhere. Under the beds. In the spare room. Stuffed away in every corner and closet. We sold all kinds of leather, all different grades of softness and strength. Heavy leather for work shoes. Crocodile and alligator for ladies. And *margosha*, the finest grade leather, with those tiny holes. Ask me anything about leather, anything! I know

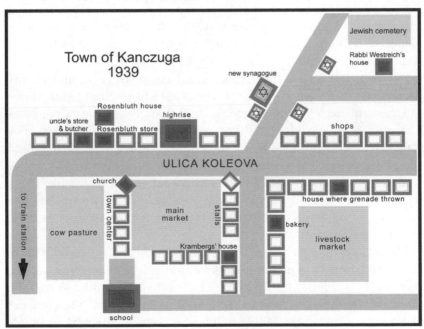

it! I know how to work as much as possible on the same piece. You've got to lay out the cardboard forms really carefully, heel to toe, then mark it out and cut out the pieces. I am very good at it.

The big wooden counter ran from one wall of the store to the other, with the merchandise piled on shelves behind it. Customers like Mr. Chmura and Mr. Zajac would ask to see the sheets of leather, and we'd lay them out on the long counter. While my parents and I schlepped down the leather, my sister Faiga kept an eye out for any peasants who forgot to pay.

I worked next to my father and mother like a grown-up. They trusted me. I could've run the store on my own, Tata said. I've got a head for business. Always have.

When I was a baby, robbers broke into our store. They ran off with most of the goods, and my parents and grandparents were tearing out their hair. I was always a sickly kid, but that night I showed my stuff. When the men were finally caught, they said they had planned to go into the house and kill our family. But, as they came close, I woke up and started to bawl. And wouldn't you know, those big, strong robbers got scared and ran away! The man of the house, at one year old!

I liked being the only son, the heir to the family name. And I looked forward to the day when I would have my own store, maybe in a bigger town. Then I would have my own servant to wait on me. And I would be respected like my father. I thought it would be great, just as long as I didn't have to be a rabbi too, and study Torah, like he did.

But then the Gypsy musicians would come to town, and all my dreams would fly away, as if they were afraid of violins or something. The peasants watched the women with the jangly earrings. Coal-black hair and long, colorful skirts that swayed with their hips when they slapped the tambourine. I'm not saying I didn't look at them, too. But I stared just as much at the men. They could have been a different animal from the Jews I knew. Their muscles burst out of their shirts like tigers trying to break free from a cage. Their eyes flashed. They were dark like us, but in a different way. Our darkness came from having no light. Theirs was dangerous.

The musicians came to town on *yarmark*, market day. And the tunes that sprang from their instruments were so alive, it was as if we could see them in the air! From the first time I heard them, I wanted to play the violin. Maybe it was because they played it, and it seemed like a way out of Kanczuga, as if I could just follow the notes to the next town. Or

20

maybe because of the way they plucked such beautiful melodies from those scraps of wood. My parents wouldn't allow it, of course. Making music wasn't fitting for an Orthodox Jewish boy.

People threw pennies into a hat the band set at the musicians' feet. I always tossed in a couple, but one at a time, so I could get close to them as much as possible. I strolled up there as if I weren't going to just stop at the hat but would actually go over and join them.

Too soon they started to pack up their things, and my heart fell. It wasn't just that I loved the music, but that they could leave and I had to stay. Who cared if you had a servant, a nice house and plenty to eat, if you weren't free? I ask you, what else is there that really matters?

# Fay

Wednesday through Friday, the peasants sold their produce, chickens, meat, and other goods to the Jewish shopkeepers and used the money to purchase whatever the Jews had for sale. But Tuesday was market day, when they were free to do their business with anyone they pleased.

The rynek sat in the center of town, surrounded by stones. The market was lined with stalls, bursting with small livestock, eggs, and milk, plump tomatoes and cabbages, pots, paper, and other household goods. It smelled of pigs and chickens. Children skipped past the merchandise, every so often stumbling and setting off an avalanche of vegetables. In the midst of it all, farmers and merchants called out to the crowd in loud, singsong voices. "Fresh potatoes! Beets like you've never seen in your life!"

My friend, also named Faiga, and I were six or seven, out on our own to enjoy the spectacle. It was one of those spring days when the air is a warm hand upon your cheek and the flowers seem to grow before your eyes. I knew the market well. When business was slow, my father sent out leather to have shoes made, then sold the shoes here. My friend's experience was somewhat different. Her parents were terribly poor. When they came to the market, they bought only what they couldn't do without.

But, that day, we were unencumbered by relations. Like little housewives, we examined the squealing pigs, begging to be released from their pens. We held our noses at the fish stall but gazed longingly at the brightly colored fabrics.

"What do you think of these potatoes?" she asked at one kiosk.

Under the watchful eye of the farmer, I reached for one and squeezed it, as I thought I'd seen my mother do. "Fair," I said. "But I think we can do better."

22

The farmer shooed us away, and we continued our trek, giggling and making faces. The market was so crowded that several times we almost lost each other in the tide.

Then Faiga said, "Look at those beautiful flower pots!"

"You're right," I said, "they're beautiful. Too bad we don't have any money. I asked my mother for some, but she was too busy with the baby."

At the mention of my brother, I made a face.

My friend grinned. "That's okay; let's steal them!"

I hesitated a second or two, then looked over at the stallkeeper. A sausage-like woman with piercing eyes, she was deep in conversation with a customer.

We each took a flowerpot and strolled off, our hearts pounding. When we were out of sight of the market, we started to run. Breathless, I reached our store and threaded my way through a knot of people, eager to show my mother my prize. She was waiting on a customer, but, out of the corner of her eye, she glanced curiously at the pot.

Our Mamche was a small woman, fine-boned and fair, with a pleasant, open face that seemed to glow from within. She wore a short, dark wig to hide her hair, as was the custom among married Jewish women of faith. Everyone respected Mamche. She had once traveled all the way to Vienna, and she knew her prayers as well as any man.

Mamche was an orphan. She was raised by her grandfather, Hersh Langsam, a scholar so revered that, when she invited him to visit when I was a little girl, she bought him a throne, a high-backed wing chair with a satin seat cushion striped in every color of the rainbow. The only time I was ever spanked was when Zayde arrived from Bucowsko and I refused to get up from his chair.

When the customer was gone, I rushed up to my mother. "Mamche," I said, "have you ever seen such a wonderful flowerpot?"

"Wonderful, yes. But where did you get such a thing?"

"I stole it at the market!" I said proudly. "Faiga got one, too!"

My mother clutched the counter for support and placed a hand on her heart. "*Vey is mir!* Woe is me! My child is a thief!"

"But—!"

"But what?" She reached for the flower pot. Reluctantly, I handed it to her. She set it down on the floor beside the counter.

"Now," she said, grabbing hold of my arm. "Come with me. Show me where you got it."

"I can do it myself!" I said, feeling my bottom lip start to tremble.

"Look, my son," she said, pulling Tunia onto her lap. "You are your father's son. You are a smart boy. You should be the best in your class, not failing math tests."

"I know, Mamche. I can't help it."

We heard a cough in the hall.

Mr. Horowitz! My mother lowered Tunia to the floor and stood up. By the time my tutor entered the room, she was smiling again, and so was I.

Mr. Horowitz was about thirty, tall and good-looking, with intense dark eyes and a thick black beard. Since I was doing so bad in the religious cheder too, my parents hired him to teach me Bible, Hebrew language, and Jewish law. My parents liked him a lot. I think they saw him as their last hope for turning me into a scholar.

"Have some *kichel*, Mr. Horowitz?" Mamche asked.

"Thank you, maybe later." He gave her a smile and a little bow.

Mamche pulled out a big steel pot from the oven. She said, "Well, then, I'll leave you two men to your work. Luzer, if Tata is looking for me, tell him I am bringing food over to Symy." Over her shoulder, she called back, "Go easy on him, Mr. Horowitz! He's had a hard day!"

I followed Mr. Horowitz into the dining room. One by one, he pulled his books from his shabby satchel and set them on the table. They were old acquaintances that had worn out their welcome, those books. The Holy Scriptures. And a Talmud, the sages' commentary to the Bible.

"Tough day?" he asked with a grin. He was always grinning. To look at him, you'd think he had the best life in the world. Yet his shoes had holes, and more than once I'd heard his stomach growl with hunger when the room was quiet.

I shrugged. "Nothing special."

"Well, since your mother is paying me, and she told me to go easy on you, I am under obligation to oblige. So—"

He reached into his bag once more and pulled out a book that looked different from the rest. It had a colorful cover instead of a plain leather binding.

"What do you say we do a novel for a change?"

That was a joke. Mr. Horowitz was always reading to me from Yiddish novels, where the girl was kidnapped and the hero came to save her before the villain had his way. They were all the same, and I ate up every word.

When the hour was up, and Mr. Horowitz packed up his books and said goodbye, I went outside. Freedom at last! I had a good group of friends, some Orthodox like me, some not. Yankele Kelstecher was my age, religious and brilliant. Willie Kromberg was also religious. His parents were rich. Yehudah Erlich was a little guy, another smart one, who planned to be a teacher.

These three were crouching in the street against a store not far from my house, playing one of our favorite games. We had these buttons in every color you could think of, and we'd lay them out on the ground. Then we'd toss coins against the wall. If your coin hit at least one of the buttons, you got to keep all of them. Then you put out more buttons and did it all over again.

Yehudah looked up at me. "Want to play, Luzer?" he asked.

I shrugged. "I don't know," I said. "My mother just gave me a talking-to about it."

"What do you mean?"

"She hates this game," I said. "So does my father, though he never says much. But Mamche asked if this is any way for a Jewish boy to spend his time."

"Did she yell at you?"

"Nah, she never yells. She just—talked. It's just as bad, when she looks so disappointed in me. She told me I could do something better with my life instead of wasting time with buttons. I think she's worried I'm going to end up like our handyman Kwasniak or something. And since she's not too happy with me right now, I'd just as soon do something else."

"So what do you want to do instead?" Yankele asked. He leaned back on his haunches in the dirt like a funny little dog.

"Well, there's always poker."

Willie looked at me like I was crazy. He said, "My parents would kill me if we did that. How about jacks?"

I nodded. "That's not so bad," I said. "Mamche isn't so against jacks. Maybe 'cause she's good at it."

Yankele's eyes widened. "Your mother plays jacks?"

"You never saw her?" Willie asked, nudging him with his elbow. "She's the best in the neighborhood!"

Yankele clapped his hand to his forehead as if now he'd seen everything. Willie ran off to get the jacks, while the rest of us fooled around with the buttons.

"Did you give Janusz the homework today?" I asked Yankele.

He nodded. "Did I have a choice? You're lucky nobody wants your homework. It's a real pain."

27

I didn't say much after that. I wanted to ask what they thought of the Polish boy Janusz's cousin, a pretty girl who was staying with him and going to school for a while. But there were some things you didn't talk about with some religious boys. Poker was one. Girls was another.

Our jacks were square little bones from a calf's leg, just the right size for picking up in your fingers. We played for a while, but I got bored pretty quick.

"What's the matter, Luzer?" Willie asked. "I thought you wanted to do this."

"I know," I said. "But I've got an idea. How'd you like to have a wagon?"

Three pairs of eyes doubled in size. I loved to get a rise out of them.

"A wagon? Where are you going to get that?"

"I'm going to make it," I said.

With my three friends trailing behind, I found some lumber and tools in our basement. In a couple of hours, I'd built a little wagon. They were amazed! Here they were so smart with their book learning; it was nice to know I could do something they couldn't.

We schlepped that wagon all over town, giving one another rides. Once we even jumped in all together, rolling down a hill and whooping the whole way. And by the time the sun went down and my wagon was safely parked in our garden, I felt good. As if nobody could ever hurt me.

# Fay

We had finished supper. Tata was studying Talmud in the bedroom, and Mamche and I were knitting at the dining room table. Everything beyond the lamp's soft glow was so shadowy that I felt as though we were sitting in an island of light in the midst of a black and desolate ocean. I could make out the swollen shapes of furniture, but, in the dark, they looked like ships, anchored in the distance.

"Faiga," Mamche said suddenly, looking up from the sweater in her lap. "Check to see that your father has tea in there, will you?"

The last thing I wanted to do was leave the light, but I didn't want to talk back to Mamche, either. Not tonight of all nights. I set down my work with a sigh. Then I stood up, navigated the few steps to the bedroom door, and poked my head in. A pot of water balanced nimbly on the little coal-burning stove.

Returning to the table, I said, "I guess Rózia already took care of it."

Mamche smiled. "Good people, those Kwasniaks. I don't know what we'd do without them. Before we had servants, it was all I could do to manage the store and the house. And now, with all these children underfoot! They're lifesavers."

I nodded, but I was not really paying attention. The Kwasniaks were fixtures of our lives; I did not think about them much. They lived next door, over the fence. They had four children. I went to school with one of the boys.

I fingered the unfinished scarf on the table. "Mamche," I said quietly. "There's something I wanted to talk to you about."

"I told you I don't want to discuss it anymore, Faiga."

"But why?" I asked. I could hear that childish whine in my voice, but I was helpless to stop it.

Mamche heard it, too. "You sound like a little girl, like Senia or Tunia."

29

I said, "Treat me like a child, I'll sound like a child."

Just then, Luzer ran into the room carrying a huge square of wood. "Mamche, look!" he cried. "Look at the sled I made!"

I frowned. "Speaking of children."

Mamche ignored me. "Luzele, that's amazing!"

Pulling the lamp over to the thing to get a better look, she asked, "You made this all by yourself?"

When he nodded, she said, "You are a brilliant child, mein nachusl. Tell me, how was school?"

From my new outpost in the shadows, I asked, "Failed any tests today?"

He frowned. "How did you know?"

"I hear things."

"Well, you're wrong," he said. "So just shut up."

"Luzer!" my mother said. "Such a way to talk to your sister!"

His happy mood had so completely deflated that I must admit I felt a little guilty. But only a little.

"I'm going next door," he said. He gave her a kiss, picked up the sled, and bounced out of the room. As he passed my chair, he pinched my upper arm, hard.

"You stupid kid!" I shouted.

"Enough, you two," my mother sighed, returning the lamp to its position and me to the light. "The Torah says that you are your brother's keeper, Faigale. Family is the most important thing there is."

My mother had a point. She was orphaned when she was five and raised by a cold-hearted stepmother. When her older brother married, he took her in for a while. After that, she lived with a cousin in Vienna and then with her grandparents. She married at sixteen, but her first husband was impotent, so the marriage was annulled. She returned to her brother's house, where she was introduced to my father.

Tata had also been married before and had had a child. His wife had died in childbirth, and their baby had been killed in one of the many pogroms in which the peasants massacred Jews.

I knew the stories well, so I also knew how hurt she was by my bickering with Luzer. But somehow I could not stop myself. We were far enough apart in age that we had nothing in common, yet close enough that we resented the attention the other got from Mamche.

"You're right," I said. "I'm sorry." Then I paused, took a breath, and added, "I saw Abraham Kunzler today."

"Hmmm, isn't he the leader of your youth group?" she asked, her lips curving into a grin.

She had such a gentle way of teasing that I found it hard to get angry. But she knew from long experience that this was one subject I was unable to joke about.

"Be serious!" I said. "This is my life!"

She put down her knitting and took my hand. "I know that, my darling. As I said before, I am just worried that you are spending so much time at your group, and they are filling you with such ideas about going to Palestine, about Palestine being the homeland of the Jews."

"I'm going there," I said. "I'm going there to live."

"I know," she said quietly. "You're an independent girl, and there's nothing I can do to stop you. But you're not going yet. First, we have to see about getting you married."

"Never!" I shouted. Then, in a calmer voice, I added, "At least not until I'm there."

"If you're not planning on getting married any time soon," she whispered, leaning close to me, "then I suggest that you stay out of those peasant dances. You don't want to get carried away."

My face burned. "I—I—But how did you—?"

She chuckled. "Never mind how I know," she said. "It's a small town. Let's just hope your father doesn't find out."

"Oh, Mamche," I said, reaching for her other hand. "Please don't tell Tata! He'd kill me!"

She gave me a searching look and shook her head. "What will we do with you, my beautiful Faigale?"

And what would I have done without Mamche, whom I disappointed again and again, because I was vain, willful, indolent and selfish? Who loved me because I was her pride and hope. Who loved me more than her life.

# Leo

It was late, and so dark that I couldn't make out my parents' bed on the other side of the room. What woke me up? Then I heard it again: the ping of stones at our store windows. Next a crash like thunder.

"Tata?" I whispered.

"He's gotten up to guard the store," Mamche said. "It's just the goyims' Good Friday, Luzele. Go back to sleep."

I hid my head under the covers, but the noise went on forever. When we woke up the next morning, Mamche and I crept out to take a look. Shattered glass covered the pavement like squished fireflies. And, just like every year, the Gentiles had hung up a huge dummy, like a scarecrow, over our door. It was beaten to pieces now. That was the game. They called the dummy *Judash*, for Jew.

I clawed at the thing, but I couldn't do much more to it than they had already done. Gently my Mamche pushed me aside, unhooked the dummy, and carried it to the trash heap.

On the way back into the house, she said, "If it gets out their anger and jealousy, Luzele, tell me, what's the harm? Would you rather they hit us for real?"

She was stroking my hair, but I shrugged her away.

Not long afterward, I was sitting at the supper table, my hands balled into fists under my chin.

My mother looked up from her plate. "What's the matter, mein nachusl?"

I shrugged. "Nothing."

"They pulled his payos again," Faiga said.

I said, "Oh, what do you know about it!"

"Bruchcia's brother Yetzel told me." She spoke in that way she had that dared me to disagree.

"Well, he doesn't know what he's talking about! So just shut up!"

"Luzer!" my father said. "Such a way to talk to your sister!"

I apologized, but I was still miserable. Here I was almost ten years old, and they'd yanked my payos so hard that I'd cried right in front of them.

"I hate them!" I said.

Mamche sighed. "My son, we are closer to God than the goyim, and they are jealous of us. What can we do?"

"We'll sure be closer to God when we're dead!"

At that she reached over and took both my hands in hers. She said, "When the Messiah comes, my dear, we will all get what we deserve. Whether we are living or dead."

"But how do you know that for sure?"

She looked at my father. He frowned and said, "How does she know? Because we are Jews, and that is what we have always known."

"If I were grown up, I'd do something about it!"

To my surprise, no one answered.

It was late summer, and although it was past dark, I was dripping with sweat. After the meal, Mamche told me to go out in the garden to cool off. Our garden was great, but after a few minutes out there alone, I got bored. I wandered over to the next-door neighbors' yard. They had a daughter about my age, and they were always pretty nice to us. Like us, they grew all kinds of vegetables—cucumbers, tomatoes, everything you could think of. I'd seen them carry water from the well across the street every day. Then they'd get down on their hands and knees in the dirt, weeding and planting. Sometimes it looked sort of as if they worshiped the earth instead of Jesus Christ.

Before I knew what I was doing, I tiptoed over, and, quiet as a robber, I ripped out their vegetables by the roots and tossed them in a heap. Worms wriggled in the moist dirt; I probably threw out a bunch of them, too. My heart pounded in my ears, but I couldn't stop.

When I was done, I tiptoed inside, washed up, and climbed into bed. Later, when Mamche came in to kiss me, I made like I was asleep.

But I was awake most of the night. My skin was crawling with excitement, as if maybe some of those little worms had followed me home. Early in the morning, while everyone was still sleeping, I climbed up to the attic. The neighbors came out soon after. From my hiding place, I watched them curse and scream and tear at their hair. The more they cried, the tougher I felt.

I saw those people all the time, and I always wondered whether they knew the truth. Maybe they were afraid to speak up. No one liked to insult my father, at least not to his face.

Seems like he lived a hundred years ago, that stupid little kid. Seems like another lifetime, all of it. All of it gone.

# Fay

On a warm Thursday afternoon in the spring of 1937, Mamche crossed the street as she did every Thursday to buy chicken and beef at the butcher shop. The butcher was my friend Luci's father, and, when business was slow during the week, he came to our family's store to chat. Luci's father always saved the best cuts of meat for Mamche, more because my mother was known for her goodness than because I was close with his daughter.

When my mother returned, I was in the kitchen, knitting a pink scarf for my sister Senia.

"That looks pretty good," she said, unwrapping the meat and laying it out on the table.

"It's okay, I guess. Not as good as you could do."

She pulled out pans and utensils, potatoes, a jar of fat and others of spices, all the while singing a Shabbos melody under her breath.

Haveinu shalom alecheim. Haveinu shalom alecheim.
Haveinu shalom aleicheim. Haveinu shalom, shalom, shalom aleichem!

"So much work for Shabbos," I said. "And it's only Thursday. All week long you work in the store, then Thursday you're up all night baking. You work so hard!"

"That's what a family is all about," she said. "You'll have one of your own pretty soon. You're seventeen years old, you know. It's time we called the *shadchen.*"

I sighed, dropped a stitch. "Mamche, what is the point of hiring a matchmaker when I'm going to Palestine anyway? What if I marry someone who doesn't want to emigrate or who doesn't want me to learn a trade?"

My mother took a deep breath and exhaled slowly. "Dear God, where

35

did I go wrong?" she said, casting her eyes toward heaven. "What's the matter with marrying and raising children here in Kanczuga? Was it such a bad life for your mother and grandmother?"

"I want to learn a trade. I want to be a gardener."

"Gottenyu! You've got a garden, a beautiful garden behind the house. Go outside and garden!"

"You don't understand! I want to be a professional! In Palestine! Why do you let me go to my youth group to learn about Zionism if you won't let me go to Palestine?"

"We have been through this. You are too young. If you still want to go to Palestine when you are nineteen, you are free to go."

"I can't wait!"

"Well, you will have to. And, in the meantime, Faigale darling, if you have no intention of marrying and want to pursue a career, you might spend a little more time on your studies and a little less on the boys!"

"Okay," I murmured. "I guess I see your point."

She turned toward me, smiling. "I'm sorry," she said, "I didn't quite hear you."

I could never be angry with her. I jumped up and gave her a hug.

Mamche was up baking until dawn, when the house smelled as though it were built out of sugar and butter and raisins instead of bricks and mortar. Her specialties were kugel, sweet noodle pudding, and kichel, light, crusty egg cookies that deliver a satisfying crunch. The big brick oven sat like a hungry monster, taking up one entire wall of the warm kitchen, demanding to be fed, just like us.

The next afternoon, as always, Mamche sent me out to deliver Shabbos challah to the needy. I stood at the kitchen door, fingering the golden braided loaves as she delivered her weekly speech.

"Remember, Faigale," she said. "No one should know it was you who brought it!"

"I know, Mamche. But why can't Luzer take it sometimes? Why is it always me?"

She shook her head. "This is a wonderful mitzvah; you should be proud to do it. Remember, if you cast bread upon the waters, it will return to you!"

"Even challah, Mamche?"

She laughed and tugged gently at my hair. "Yes, my darling, even challah. Braided just like you."

I did not relish this chore, but it was something I'd done as long as I could remember. I walked to the shacks and the rented rooms of the poorest Jews in town and dropped off my Shabbos loaves before they came to the door. Most of the Jews in Kanczuga can barely scrape out a few *złotys* to buy themselves a chicken each week. Most of them are shopkeepers, but sometimes only two or three people come into their stores all day. One woman we know sells fresh rolls every morning, door-to-door. When her husband died, she was so poor that she didn't have enough money to bury him, and Father had to take up a collection for her. In their homes, these people have a little table knocked together from boards, a few chairs they made themselves. But, to the peasants, they are the Jewish merchant class, the elite.

When I returned from my rounds, I carried our cholent to the bakery out by the *mały rynek*, the smaller of the two farmers' markets in town. Cholent is a stew of heavily seasoned meat, beans, barley, onions, carrots, and potatoes. It is made before Shabbos and must sit in a hot oven all night, until by Saturday afternoon it is so thick you can stand a spoon in it. It is so thick that a popular joke went: Someone once asked a doctor what was the biggest miracle for the Jews? And he answered, if they go to sleep after eating cholent and wake up the next morning, it's a miracle. Because religious Jews like us weren't allowed to light an oven on Shabbos, we carried the heavy enamel pot to the bakery ahead of time, where the big oven stayed hot for twenty-four hours without relighting.

By Friday evening, we stood scrubbed and freshly dressed as Mamche lit the candles for Shabbos. One, two, three, four for us children and two more in the big silver candlesticks that came from my great-grandparents.

My father and my brother returned from shul a little later than usual. After the service, they had to comb the streets for some needy person to bring home for the Shabbos meal, because otherwise my mother would have been seriously disappointed. That night, we hosted an out-of-town guest, a beggar whom they found in the main square.

As the man of the house, Tata recited the Kiddush.

Baruch atah adonai, elohaynu melech ha'olam, boray p'ri hagafen

[Blessed art Thou, oh Lord our God, who has created the fruit of the vine].

We stood at our places around the big wooden table, our hair gleaming and our mouths watering at the succulent odors from the kitchen. Both Tata and our guest were reverential and serious, but the rest of us had to struggle not to catch each other's eyes and giggle. Luzer reached

37

for something on the table when he thought no one was looking. I pinched him, hard, and he squealed. Even Mamche, exhausted as she was, couldn't stop grinning. We were welcoming the Sabbath, and that was cause for celebration, week after week. We sang the *z'mirot* with gusto, especially our cousin Motti, who had a beautiful tenor.

We slept a little later the next morning, but only a little, because we didn't want to miss a minute of the wonderful day. The goyim were in school, but we could not attend on Shabbos. While Tata visited his family next door, Mamche sat and sang with us in the garden, so full of joy that we could never get enough, even when her songs were filled with melancholy.

Mayn kind, mayn treyst, du forst avek,
Ze zay a zun a guter,
Dikh bet mit trern un mit shrek
Dayn traye libe muter.
Du forst, mayn kind, mayn eyntsik kind,
Ariber vayte yamen
Akh kum ahin nor frish gezunt
Un nit farges dayn mamen.
Yo! for gezunt un kum mit glik,
Ze yede vokh a brivil shik,
Dayn mames harts, mayn kind, derkvik.

[My child, my comfort, you are going across distant seas.
Arrive in good health and write each week
To ease your mother's worries.
Write a letter soon, my child.
Your mother will read your letter and be comforted.
Ease her pain, her bitter heart, refresh her spirit.]

"Faiga, I have an idea," my mother said suddenly.

I looked up from braiding Senia's long, blond hair. "*Nu*, what is it?" I asked.

"You know we have a customer, a wealthy Gentile who owns an experimental garden on his land. Once a year, they come to our store to order leather for their employees' shoes."

"Yes, I know who you mean."

"Well, they told us to expect them this week. And I was thinking, maybe you can learn from them how to become a professional gardener."

"Oh, Mamche! That would be fantastic!" Dropping Senia off my lap so quickly that she cried out in alarm, I ran over to hug my mother. "I love you so much," I said.

"I love you too, my beautiful Faigale."

Not to be outdone, Luzer and Senia and Tunia rushed over, and we all surrounded my mother, holding her close.

Baby Tunia said, "You can't love us as much as we love you, Mamche, because there are four of us children, and just one of you."

We laughed, all except our mother, who scooped us in her arms like so many sheaves of wheat and held onto us as if she'd never let us go.

A few days later, the rich man's wife came into our store, with her big German shepherd on a leash by her side. When I asked her whether I might work in her garden, she agreed immediately and scribbled a quick note of introduction for the manager.

I visited the garden a few times. It was a magical place, a misty world of colors and textures so beautiful and exotic it was almost painful. They grew vegetables and flowers from seeds collected all over the world, and I used to bring Mamche bunches of fresh asparagus and armloads of pink and purple flowers.

But my fingernails were always filthy, and my back and knees ached from bending in the soil. Just as bad, the heat left me parched and panting, like an old dog.

I came to realize that gardening wasn't all that desirable a profession after all. So my parents sent me to Przemyśl to live with my mother's brother, and there I attended a trade school to learn to be a seamstress. I loved the cosmopolitan city, with its beautiful, wide River San and its fancy shops. My uncle was president of the Jewish Hospital, and his family owned the ironworks. They had a wonderful house and knew everyone who was anyone. After class, I helped take care of my cousins, sweet girls about my sisters' ages.

I did not mind cutting out the patterns and learning the trade. But, within the year, I returned home. I wanted to build a better world. How to do that as a seamstress? How to do that in Kanczuga? If only, I thought, lying once again with my sisters in that cramped little bed and gazing up at the ceiling, if only I could get out of this town for good.

# Leo

I was hanging around outside the store one day when one of our customers pulled up on his bicycle. Wow! I let out a low whistle at the sight of it. It was a black ladies' bicycle, nothing special. But, to me, it was much more. As the man jumped off and leaned it against the wall, he caught me watching him.

"Mr. Luzer Rosenbluth," he said. "How are you today?"

"Fine," I said, kicking up dust with my shoes. "Nice bicycle."

I felt my face get hot; he must have seen it. He said, "You don't have a bicycle?"

I looked at my feet. My black shoes were now covered with white dust, as if they'd been specially powdered.

"My parents won't allow it," I said. "They say religious Jewish boys don't ride bicycles."

"Well," the man said, folded his cap and putting it into his coat pocket, "I don't know what religious Jewish boys do or don't do, because I'm Catholic. But if you want to try out this bicycle while I'm inside, it's fine with me."

Fighting to keep my voice even, I said, "You mean it?" Like a squeak it came out, and the man laughed.

"Of course I mean it. Why don't you take it over to that field over there, on the grass? That way if you fall, you won't hurt yourself."

"I won't fall!" I promised, reaching for the handlebars.

"You know how to ride a bicycle?" he asked doubtfully.

"Oh, sure! My friend lets me ride his all the time!"

As if to call me a liar, the thing bucked the minute I jumped on. But I quickly righted myself and was on my way.

"Be back in half an hour!" the man called, laughing. "And don't hit any cows!"

In fact, I'd only ridden a bicycle once before. But, without a backward glance, I raced to the field, my payos flying. I rode faster and faster through the grass. Scattering birds and cows with the squall of my bell. Nearly washing out as I rounded the turn at the end of the field. And all the time thinking, if this was what it meant to be nonreligious, it was okay by me.

# Fay

After lunch one Shabbos, my friends and I headed as usual for the railroad station. We strode down the street with our arms linked, three and four abreast, clopping our fashionable high heels on the paving stones. On the Sabbath, Jewish activity was severely restricted. No writing, no listening to the gramophone or using electricity. Yet what wonderful freedom we enjoyed on that day, so young and pretty and dressed to kill!

Bruchcia and Runia and Chajka were there, and so was the rest of our group. Genendla's father was our Rabbi Westreich. I had seen Genendla almost every day since we were born. I was like another daughter to her parents, which was quite an honor, because a rabbi's daughter cannot be friends with just anybody. Genendla had a beautiful voice, and she was lively and smart, as were her seven brothers and sisters.

Malka was the opposite. One of six children, she was fragile in body and spirit. Faiga had the same name I do, but she was raised very differently. Despite the incident with the flowerpots, my father always pointed to Faiga as an example to me. If you were as smart as she, you could go to college, he would tell me. Faiga was too poor to attend.

Gittel's parents were our competitors in the leather business, but that didn't affect our friendship. For one thing, they weren't very successful at it. She was quiet and homely, one of six daughters. But, to me, she was very special, one of my dear, dear friends.

When we arrived at the station, we headed for a corner of the platform far from the passengers on their way to Dynów and Przeworsk. There we sang and danced the tango and foxtrot, just as if it were our own private stage. We mimicked the Polish singers we heard on Bruchcia's gramophone, and we made up tunes of our own. Songs of love gone wrong, of dreamy-eyed boys and happy times. No one paid much attention to us. We had long ago become a Saturday afternoon tradition.

Come the first stars in the sky, we were off to our Gentile classmates' homes to find out what we had missed in school that day. They were always so jealous that we had Saturdays off. They never thought how hard it was to miss one day of school each week, whether we wanted to or not. But I did not tell them that. I acted as if it were a special gift set aside for the Chosen People.

On Sunday, Bruchcia, Chajka, Runia, and I sneaked into a peasant festival. Sometimes the parties were held in one of the villages that ring our town, but, that night, it was on the ground floor of a building right on the Kolejova. The fiddlers and accordion players tap-tapped their toes to the beat, and my friends and I polkaed for hours, until our feet were rubbed raw in our fancy high heels.

We knew everyone there, and everyone knew us, from the store, the village, or other parties. One of the boys, a good-looking farmer with bulging muscles and a mass of freckles, asked me to be his partner almost every dance. I had seen him at these festivals several times before, and he was always pleasant and respectful. All the girls wanted to dance with him.

As the evening progressed, he held me closer and closer, nuzzling my cheek with his. We'd been dancing for hours, but he still smelled like the outdoors.

I was shaking so hard; I don't know what I would have done if he'd tried to kiss me. I'd never done that before. All I kept hearing were my mother's words: A Jewish girl must be different. She must value herself and not become too free before marriage, or she will never find a respectable husband.

Of course, that would never happen to me. But what could be the harm in dancing? If that was the only way I could be near a man, especially a handsome goy, then I would dance until my feet fell off.

I had heard the whispers about a Jewish girl in Pruchnik, a village not far from us. She fell in love with her Gentile music teacher. They married and ran away together, and her parents never wanted to see her again. For them, she was dead. They even sat shivah, the seven-day ritual of mourning.

I agreed with Mamche that that was terrible, and I did want to be a good girl. But Mamche was not dancing in the arms of the best-looking boy at a party. It was all I could do not to swoon.

We were the only Jews at these gatherings, but nobody seemed to mind, least of all our handsome partners. "We don't like Jews," they told us, "but we like you." And when we were with them, they were so attentive and kind that we were hard-pressed to discover any difference between us at all.

# Leo

Spring was Pesach time, when we celebrated the release of the Jewish slaves from Egypt. As if we had personally been freed—that was how we were supposed to feel, the whole eight days. The first night, the family sat around the table for the Passover Seder, the special dinner where we tell the story of the holiday. The Seder went on for hours, which you'd think would drive us kids nuts. But we got lots of special treats and extra attention, especially during the search for the *afikomen*, the half slice of matzoh that Tata hid during the meal. Whoever found the afikomen got to sell it back to him. And, you know that, being the kids of a good businessman, we didn't let him off easy.

The thing about Passover is that, for eight days, you can't eat bread, noodles or anything with regular flour or yeast. You use different pots and dishes than you do the rest of the year, and the women clean the house from top to bottom.

Mamche was like a crazy woman every Pesach. You wouldn't think the house could get any cleaner than it did on Shabbos, but she and Faiga turned the place upside down. Even my little sisters helped. The rugs were beaten, the floors were washed, the kitchen was taken apart. Then came all the cooking and baking. We couldn't eat normal cakes or cookies that week, but we got lots of treats made from matzoh flour. And to make things rise without yeast, you needed eggs. Dozens and dozens of them. With cakes that took six eggs to rise, Jews kept the chickens busy that time of year. We also ate the eggs alone. By the end of that long week, we all looked a little like eggs ourselves. White and rounded, if you know what I mean.

The year I turned eleven, Passover started out like any other, with my exhausted mother working around the clock. Then one night, I woke up screaming. I felt as if someone were cutting out my insides with one of Mamche's carving knives.

Somebody called for the doctor, and he came right over. As for me, I couldn't've stopped crying if my life depended on it. The doctor said I had appendicitis. He told my parents that if I didn't go to the hospital and get my appendix taken out, it could burst. I pictured pieces of me all over the room and cried all the harder.

Mamche helped me dress, while Tata found someone to take us over to the hospital in Przemyśl. Even Faiga was nice to me, telling me to get better as fast as I could.

The ride took a couple of hours. The whole way, I was in agony. What a waste! Here I had my mother all to myself on a trip to the city, and I couldn't even enjoy it!

Mamche's cousin Shaye was president of the biggest hospital in the city, which helped me get in right away. The doctor was a distinguished-looking guy, with silver hair and a face deeply lined like a road map. When my mother saw him, she said, "Doctor, I don't mean to offend you, but this boy is my life. He means everything to us. If you feel there's any-body better than you—"

So amazed was I at Mamche's chutzpah, I almost forgot my pain. But the doctor just bowed and said, "Madam, if you would blindfold me, I could perform the operation perfectly. Since I won't be blindfolded, I'll do even better."

My mother was satisfied, and they operated that night. When I woke up in the hospital room, the sun was shining through the window like a bonfire, and Mamche was holding my hand.

"Well, hello there," she said, her eyes crinkling with pleasure. "Nice to have you back! I was getting a little bored, sitting here looking at you!"

"Where—?"

"You're in the hospital in Przemyśl, in your own beautiful private room. And your Mamche is going to stay with you until you're ready to go home."

I was glad, but I was too weak to show it. I squeezed her hand.

Mamche reached for a damp cloth from the nightstand and wiped my forehead. She said, "You'll never guess what the doctor said caused the trouble! Eggs! A piece of eggshell was stuck in your appendix!"

Again I squeezed.

"Well, Luzele," she said. "You need your rest. Try to go back to sleep."

"How long?" I whispered.

"We won't be here too long, mein nachusl. A few days, maybe."

Two days later, the incision burst. They fitted me with a tube to drain the pus. The odor was horrible, a disgusting mixture of old cheese and, what a surprise, rotten eggs. But even worse was the torture on my mother's face. The smell would've been enough to do that to her. But it was the fear. When she wasn't pacing the room, she was davening from her little prayerbook.

Sometime during that period she must have slept on the spare bed, but I never saw it. Every time I opened my eyes, she was awake, smiling down at me and holding my hand.

When I was feeling a little better, Mamche went out and bought me some sweets. One day, the nurse even brought me a cup of coffee with milk and sugar. How lucky adults were to drink this every day! Not for the first time, I couldn't wait to grow up.

# Leo

"**H**ey, Luzer! Wait for me!"
      A few more steps I trudged between the snow drifts, not wanting to stop. I felt that if I did, I wouldn't be able to get myself started again. So fierce was the wind that it brought tears to my eyes. My breath in front of my face looked like smoke from a pipe. I had gloves, but, for all the feeling in my fingers, they might as well have been on someone else.

Still I couldn't ignore Henek, so I stopped and waited for him to catch up.

When my friend reached me, he was puffing like a steam engine. He said, "I was thinking you might want to go get some kielbasa."

Just the word was enough to give me a funny feeling in my stomach. Pigs were *treyf*, forbidden for Jews to eat. And pork sausage was about as treyf as you could get. I had never tasted kielbasa. While we're at it, I had never tasted treyf of any kind. What, I always wondered, was I missing? What was so great about this stuff that it was a sin to eat?

When I didn't say anything, he sneered. "Don't tell me you're scared! Just because it's made of a little old pig."

"If my parents found out—"

He shrugged. "What would they do to you? Disown you? Kill you? You're their ben yahid. You could get away with murder."

I sighed. "Murder, maybe. Eating kielbasa, I'm not so sure."

"Oh, come on," he said, stamping his feet in the snow to keep warm. "I don't have all day. What do you say?"

I thought it over. Henek was one of the smartest boys in the class. I should be more like him, my parents were always saying. It sounded like a weak argument, even to me. But my mouth was already watering. I'd smelled those kielbasa stalls. If the taste was anything like the smell, I was in.

48

"Oh, okay," I said. "Let's go."

His grin filled maybe half his face. He said, "Okay!"

Now that I'd decided, I wanted to get it over with—fast. We tramped through the snow. The air was so sharp, stinging our lungs. I tried to imagine what kielbasa tasted like. If only I could have gotten the sound of my mother's voice out of my head! Or maybe it was the wind.

Finally we reached the peasant's stall on the edge of the rynek. When we ducked inside, I realized that all along I'd been half-hoping it would be closed. The place reeked of roasting meat. Henek pulled out a coin and handed it to the old man. He got a long, thick sausage that spit and sizzled on his plate like a rattlesnake.

I watched him take a bite, saw the blood dribble down his chin. Then I felt the man's eyes on me.

I reached for my money, but my hand froze in my pocket.

"What's the matter?" Henek asked, his mouth full. "You need to borrow a few złotys?"

My belly filled with butterflies, as if I'd been called on to answer a math question in school. The old peasant looked from my friend to me. I gave them both a weird kind of smile.

I said, "What I need to borrow is a new family."

He shook his head. "I don't get it."

I swallowed hard. Even then, my stomach growled for that sausage.

At last I said, "Even if I can hide from God, I can't hide from the neighbors. My parents would find out. And tonight is Shabbos. I just can't do it."

Henek screwed up his face in disgust. "Boy, you don't know what you're missing." He finished off half the sausage in one bite.

I sighed and said, "I know."

When Henek finished eating, we went to my house and pulled out the wooden sled I'd made the year before. We dragged it to the big hill in the center of town, where about a dozen kids were already sledding. After a while, the hard-packed snow melted to slush. Back in my house again, we warmed ourselves by the stove. Then we sledded some more in the backyard.

Later, I walked with Tata to shul, just as we did every Friday at dusk. He wore his *shtreimel*, the hat with the wide brim trimmed in mink, a long coat made of silk, and another on top of it, lined with mink and with a mink collar. As usual, Tata was lost in prayer or scholarly thoughts. But it didn't matter. I felt proud, marching beside him into the old shul, taking our seats by the eastern wall that my grandfather had bought long ago.

Before the service, Tata left me for a couple of minutes while he scoured the place for a beggar to bring home for Shabbos dinner. Then he talked with the other men about the news of the day. It was a sin to talk about business or worldly things on Shabbos, but sometimes, *frum* as they were, they couldn't help themselves. I didn't know much about it, but it was as though the things the Nazis were doing in Germany always won out over everything else. Kind of like a royal flush in poker.

Then the service began, and together we sang the traditional melody:

L'cha dodi, likrat kallah, p'nai Shabbat n'kabbalah.

[Come my beloved, to welcome the Sabbath bride.]

When it was over, Tata leaned down, shook my hand and wished me *gut Shabbos*. And at that moment, kielbasa was the furthest thing from my mind.

# Fay

It was August 1939. My parents refused to buy a radio, so I always listened to the one at Bruchcia's house. Her family was known for having all the latest inventions. It was Bruchcia's brother Piniu who first hooked up electricity in Kanczuga. They even had one of those gramophones with the horn where the sound comes out. We would go there and dance the tango and the foxtrot to her Polish records.

The radio was a big square brown box that sat on the floor, and we stared at it as if it were a person speaking. My friends and I had never paid much attention to the news before, and I had always considered the radio a source of pleasure, rather than information. But, that evening, the box told us that the Polish army was mobilizing against a German attack and that the American President Roosevelt, the Belgian King Leopold, and Pope Pius XII were appealing for a peaceable settlement.

We listened to Adolf Hitler urging the Poles to surrender. He spoke a clipped, harsh German, but his words were translated into softer Polish. After the broadcast, we chatted halfheartedly about going dancing that weekend and gossiped about friends in our youth group. Bruchcia's mother served us *babka*, but I could only nibble at the sugary crust. My throat and stomach felt constricted and sour, as though I had swallowed those ugly words rather than simply listened to them.

On September 1, Hitler ignored the warnings from Britain and France and sent his army into Poland in an undeclared war. Ours was a fairly large country, with an army of more than a million and three million reserves. But our air force was small. Even worse, our entire territory was within easy striking distance of the German bombers.

After that evening, we listened to nothing but news. When a spy planted in Poland told the Nazis the locations of munitions dumps and other strategic military objectives, the rest was easy for them. Our country was crushed within a few weeks. Soviet troops poured into the east, in accordance with the terms of a Nazi–Soviet pact that we learned had been made a decade earlier. Our President Mościcki, along with Foreign Minister Beck and Marshall Rydz, fled to Romania.

And we in Kanczuga braced for the worst.

# Fay

At the beginning of the war, Jews were allowed to travel freely. Tradesmen and relatives passed through town, faces knotted with fear and telling the most terrible stories. We did not know whether to turn away or to beg for more, and, more often than not, we did both. Germany was occupying all of Europe, they told us, snatching from their beds those Jews who hadn't managed to escape, rounding them up like cattle and shooting them like dogs.

Ironically, the events that were tearing apart so many families brought ours closer together, at least at first. When the Germans invaded our country, my father's youngest brother, Sruly, and his family came from far-off Krynica, where he had married and opened a fancy shoe store. Krynica was the most expensive resort in Poland, and Uncle Sruly had a good business, a wife, and three young children.

Sruly was in his forties at the time, a slender man with an irrepressible smile, a clean-shaven face—unheard of for an observant Jew—and a love of life that was truly infectious. He was my favorite uncle, and I was his favorite, too. Every summer I spent several weeks with him in Krynica while his wife and family vacationed at another resort. I always thought those visits were the perfect combination of being both a spoiled child and an independent adult. And every year, he weighed me down with expensive gifts to take back home to my family.

They arrived one afternoon in an elegant horse and carriage, in a flurry of trunks and hat boxes, with shoes and scraps of leather to sell along the way. I didn't know where to look first. Eagerly I watched my aunt unpack her elegant dresses in the latest styles from Paris. But, every few minutes, I would run over to wherever Uncle Sruly was, just to see him, just to take comfort in the fact that he was close by.

At the same time, our wealthy cousin Yossi Kneller came to us with his wife and three children. His town was rich in oil wells, and he was quite successful in the oil business, young, handsome, and religious in a modern way, meaning, mainly, that he kept his beard trimmed short.

The men were still allowed to make a living, while for us females, those early days of the war were filled with more housework than we'd ever done in their lives. Mamche, her sisters-in-law, and I had more than twenty people to cook and clean for, and the tumult at mealtimes was enough to keep all of our mind off our troubles.

Still, we knew that we were lucky. Every other family we talked to was already missing someone, either because the relative had been sent to Siberia or because the person was already dead. In the evenings, we gathered with our closest neighbors, taking hope in any spark of good news and praying for a miracle. Maybe they'll forget about us, our neighbor would say. Frightened as we were, we still found things to give us pleasure. Especially when Mamche sang, the war felt very far away.

Shteyt zikh dort in gesele
Shtil fartrakht a hayzele,
Drinen oyfn boydem-shtibl
Voynt mayn tayer Reyzele.
Yedn ovnt farn hayzl
Drey ikh zikh arum,
Kh'gib a fayf, un ruf oys: "Reyzl,
Kum, kum, kum!"

[In a quiet street,
In the attic of a little house,
Lives my dear Reyzele.
Every evening I pass under her window,
Whistle and call her to come out.
A window opens,
The old house awakens,
And Reyzele's sweet voice is heard:
"Wait a little, my dear.
I shall soon be ready.
Walk around the street a while."

Cheerfully I walk,
Singing and cracking nuts,
Listening to the patter of her little feet
Skipping down the steps.
I embrace her,
Kiss her warmly and say, "Come."]

# Leo

---

Of the Polish army, all we'd seen was pictures. So when they came to our town in the fall of 1939, we all lined up to watch. It was something to see! Some of them came on horses, towing wooden wagons that thundered across the paving stones. The foot soldiers followed, sometimes marching back and forth, other times wandering around, it seemed, in aimless circles. They stood tall in their golden uniforms and shiny black boots. But somehow they didn't seem like soldiers. At least not like the ones I'd imagined when I played army with my friends.

After a few hours, the soldiers went away, and we went back to the store. No customers came in. The streets were so quiet, it could've been midnight.

And then, like the roar of the devil, came the engines. The Nazis burst into our town driving these black Mercedes sedans and shiny motorcycles. This time, no one wanted to go out to watch, not even the goyim. We stood by the windows, hidden behind curtains and shades. We had heard that Jews were being persecuted in Germany and denied many jobs and even, in some places, the right to buy bread and milk.

That night, the men in our family sat up late into the night, drinking dark tea at the kitchen table and talking about the war. They were so worried that they didn't even notice when I stayed to listen.

"No good will come of this," Tata said, setting down his glass of schnapps.

Uncle Sruly said, "We don't know that for a fact. Poland has been split in two: the Soviet side to the east of the River San, the Nazi-ruled side where we are, to the west. The Russians have nothing special against the Jews."

"What about that mayor of yours?" asked cousin Yossi. "Didn't you say he would protect us?"

My father shrugged. "Dr. Sawicki is a good man, an educated man," he said, "and he has always been kind to the Jews. God willing, he will protect us."

"God willing!" said Uncle Sruly, raising his cup.

They all toasted *l'hayim* and clinked their glasses. I couldn't help noticing that their call to life was not so spirited as in days gone by.

The next morning, we kids huddled around Mamche, not knowing what else to do. When Tata came in for breakfast, our mouths fell open. Dark circles blurred his eyes like purple thumbprints, and, overnight, his beard had turned cloudy white. Mamche said later that he'd had the same blank expression on his face the day his mother died.

When Tata started to cry, standing there in the doorway, Faiga jumped up, like a puppet or something. I followed her to see where she was going. She ran past him to the bedroom, threw herself on the bed, and buried her face in her pillow. Mamche went in and folded her in her arms, weeping.

In two days, the Nazis took over the nicest buildings in town. They stormed house after house, looking for men with beards—meaning Jews—to send to work. Soon they came to ours. Tata was hidden, but, since I was just a kid, I was out playing in the street. One of the soldiers pointed to me and, in bad Polish, told me to follow him, that he had work for me to do. I was so scared, I thought I was going to be sick. But he didn't have to tell me twice. Quick as I could, I fell into step with them.

Mamche had just looked out the window when she saw them leading me away. She ran into the street, apron strings flying.

"Please, sir!" she cried out. "He is just a child. He is only thirteen."

The soldier didn't say a word. He just pushed her aside and grabbed me by the shoulder. I was so scared, I didn't dare look back.

Mamche followed us through the streets to the schoolhouse. There she watched me and other Jewish boys hauling and hammering furniture to convert the schoolhouse into barracks for the German soldiers. The work wasn't hard, and they treated us okay, I guess. But I was shaking the whole time.

When I came home that night, the family was already making plans.

# Fay

By the spring of 1940, every Jewish household in Kanczuga was discussing the same question: Would it be safer on the eastern side of our beautiful San River, which was occupied by the Russians? You could walk from house to house and pick up the same conversation, as if it were a feather in the wind:

> "The Russians have never been our friends."
> "Yes, but the leaders of the Russian Revolution were Jewish."
> "They've arrested people."
> "True, but what will the Nazis do to us?"
> "Our mayor will keep us safe."
> "But for how long can he protect us?"
> "Only the men are in danger here."
> "Do you want to leave your family behind at such a time?"

At last my parents decided to send Luzer and me to the Russian side, into Przemyśl, which we both knew so well and where we could stay with her brother, who was also named Luzer. My brother had to be kept safe above all else, and I was to be his protector. Although I wished my mother were going with me instead, I did not question the plan. By that time, I was well used to my brother's special treatment. And, besides, it was an adventure. Our cousin Yossi and Uncle Sruly would accompany us, leaving their families with ours.

In order to make the trip, we needed travel documents. So one morning, I dressed myself with extra care and set off to Dr. Sawicki's mansion at the edge of town. Our distinguished mayor was a middle-aged man with a wide girth and a gentle heart. He was known in the region as that rare public official who gave money to the poor instead of only taking it back in taxes.

The maid escorted me into the library, a room with high ceilings, ornate furniture, and row after row of leather-bound books. When I entered, Dr. Sawicki was standing with his back to me, staring out the window behind his desk.

I coughed, and he motioned me over to him, without turning around.

"Come in, child," he murmured. "How are your parents?"

"Fine, sir."

"Good, good. And what can I do for you?"

I crossed the floor and joined him at the window. The autumn sky looked like a tranquil lake, with clouds for lily pads.

"Please, Dr. Sawicki, four of us from my family would like to cross to the Russian side as soon as possible. But we need papers."

He was silent for several seconds. Holding my breath, I gazed at the gleaming lamps and the sparkling wood floors. The room smelled of furniture polish and smoke. I wondered whether he had read all the books on those shelves.

Just then several planes roared by. The noise was so loud and unexpected that I jumped and covered my ears.

He dropped one huge hand onto my shoulder and pointed with the other.

"You see, Miss Faiga Rosenbluth, those are German planes out there. We have been an island unto ourselves until now. All of the nearby towns have long since evacuated their Jews. Only Kanczuga has given ours permission to stay."

He made a fist, looked down at it sadly.

"But, as the English poet says, no man, and no town in Poland, is an island. The Germans are losing their patience with your fat mayor. I can feel it."

He turned to face me, this time placing both hands on my shoulders.

He said, "You'll get your papers, little one. God bless you and your family."

When I returned home, everyone was busy. Luzer and Yossi were making canvas rucksacks for the trip. Mamche, Rózia Kwasniak, and the rest of the women were planning what foods would be best for us to carry. My father was talking with a man about transporting us in his wagon. I gave them my news and went into the bedroom to decide what to take with me. In the back of my mind, I knew that this might be the last time I'd ever see my home. But I could not make myself believe it. I felt as though we were simply preparing for a trip. Not so long before, I had dreamed of adventure. Now, perhaps, I would finally have some. And with my uncle and cousin with us, what could happen?

I came upon a photograph of my friends, all of us together, smiling as if we would never be anything but seventeen and happy. It was the thought of my friends that made me grasp the full reality of what we were about to do. My greatest regret was that I could not say goodbye to them. But I had promised my family not to tell anyone that we were leaving. As I held the photograph in my hand, Chajka's face grew muddy and indistinct, as if she were crying. It took me a second or two to realize that the tears were mine.

On the morning we left, Mamche woke us long before dawn. I sat at the old kitchen table, memorizing every detail: the brick oven that filled an entire wall, the smells of fresh cake and strong coffee, the set of her shoulders as she moved around the room. Then I closed my eyes and listened. I heard bird calls, the voices of mothers, perhaps, teaching their little ones to fly. There was the scrape of a chair leg along the wooden floor, the clink of a spoon against a bowl. I fought back a sob. I had never paid attention to these things before. I had never listened closely enough. Now, I never wanted the moment to end.

After breakfast, Luzer and I returned to the bedroom. Senia and Tunia were still in bed. My brother and I bent down to hug their sweet-smelling bodies and pat their soft curls.

Then Tata called us back to the kitchen so that he could bless us.

Y'varekh'kha Adonai v'yishm'rekha.
Ya'er Adonai panav elekha vihuneka.
Yisa Adonai panav elekha v'yasem l'kha shalom.

[May the Lord bless you and watch over you.
May the Lord cause His face to shine upon you and be gracious to you.
May the Lord lift up His face toward you and give you peace.]

He kissed each of us solemnly, on both cheeks, and left the room.

When he was gone, Mamche took us into her arms. She held us so long without speaking that Luzer began to squirm. I heard the clop of hooves and the sad squeal of wheels coming to a stop on the pavement outside.

"We have to go now," I whispered.

She released our bodies, but her fingers held fast to our clothing. Her face was pale as ash, her eyes glassy.

"I know," she said. "You have to go. Take care, my darlings."

Luzer nodded. When I nudged his elbow, he said, "Of course, Mamche."

I bristled a little at her words, then quickly caught myself. This was no time to be jealous of my brother. I said, "We will both survive."

"Promise me," she said, nodding slowly.

Luzer and I exchanged glances. "We promise," he said.

My eyes filled with tears. "We'll do anything you want, Mamche."

At this, she broke into a smile and stroked my head. "Well," she said, "that would be a first, my darling, now wouldn't it?"

# Fay

I had pictured traveling to Przemyśl in a grand carriage, but waiting for us at the door was a skinny, bow-legged horse pulling a big wooden box normally used for transporting chickens and produce to market. Two men from the neighborhood were already sitting inside when Luzer and I climbed up. One of them was our next-door neighbor, Mr. Turm, who had left behind his wife, Elka, and their little girl, just three years old. We nodded terse hellos and knelt down in the hay, turning our faces to our families below. Uncle Sruly's and Yossi's children were sobbing at the door, holding onto their fathers' legs.

One of them cried, "Why is Daddy leaving?"

"To be safe," my aunt told her. "To keep himself safe."

Long after we rolled down the town's main road, Luzer and I gazed out the back of the wagon, as if to catch just one last glimpse of home. Then the sun rose, as it did every morning of our lives, as it would do long after we were gone. The day was beautiful, crisp and clear, with a sapphire sky and billowing clouds that looked soft as featherbeds.

We bumped along poorly paved and dirt roads for several hours. The wagon was cramped, and the least shifting of numb limbs earned an irritated glare from our fellow passengers. Luzer and I kept snapping at each other, although whether out of habit or agitation I could not say. We were certainly upset. Either we were doing the smartest possible thing to save our lives, or our father had paid to have us dragged full speed into the abyss. We had no way of knowing, and no way to pass the time, it seemed, but to anticipate the worst.

Silently I began to pray, not the five-thousand-year-old words of my people, but the worries that were in my heart: Oh God, help us pass the border alive. Help me keep my brother safe.

"Praying for my brother?" The words came out before I had had time to think of them. When I shook my head in surprise, I felt him look up, but I did not meet his gaze.

A few kilometers before we reached the river, the wagon came to an abrupt stop. Two SS men—already the most hated and feared of any German soldier—blocked our way, pistols in hand. In broken Polish, they told us to get out of the wagon, take our bags, and follow them. As quickly as possible, we six did what we were told. Our driver was already urging his horse back to town before the last of us had stepped down. We could not blame him. He had fulfilled his obligation. Without a backward glance, we followed the soldiers through some low bushes to a clearing. There we saw many people already queuing up, men in one line, women in the other.

So this was it. They were going to shoot us after all. Why had we not stayed with our mother and father? At least we could have all died together.

"Yossi," my uncle whispered. "I thought there wasn't supposed to be a patrol here."

"Evidently," said Yossi, "we were brought to the wrong place. The regular army wouldn't have bothered us. It's the SS who shoot first and ask questions later."

"Do you think we were brought here on purpose?" I asked.

Before anyone could respond, the younger of the SS men was shouting. "Listen me," he said. "Down belongings and get in proper line."

My uncle had a beautiful new umbrella that he had brought with him from Krynica. I saw him stare at it, rolling the expensive black silk in his hands. At last, he dropped it on the pile with our rucksacks and joined the other men, shaking his head, his face tight with fury.

"Now," said the SS man, "we want you give your money. Everything, jewelry, watches, whatever of value."

At any other time, the sound of this pidgin Polish would have made us smile. But even Luzer's face was screwed up, as though he would burst into tears at any moment. I wanted to run to him, but he was standing safe between my uncle and cousin. It was I who was alone in the women's line, watching the sobbing mothers and daughters with a mix of envy and disdain.

The soldiers slowly made their way down the rows with burlap sacks, and we dropped what little security we had into them. I did not even notice what I put in, so frightened was I of what was to come.

"Now, hands raise!"

The sky started to whirl around me. Either God was showing his anger, I decided, or I was going to faint. So this is what it is to die, I thought. I looked over at Luzer to say goodbye.

But what was this? They were searching his pockets for more valuables. When the man came to me, I flinched. My first time touched like this by a man, I thought ruefully. For this I have saved myself? He was not disrespectful. Nevertheless, I was glad I hadn't thought to keep anything back.

"Now," said the young man, when the search was complete. "Pick up bags; march to river."

My uncle and I looked and each other. Could it possibly be over? He shrugged and shook his head. His expression said: We will see.

Still in two lines, we marched the short distance to the river's edge. When we reached the bank, the soldier said, "Now, go!"

Go? We had expected to cross in boats! We looked from the soldiers to one another and back to the soldiers in dismay. From the set of their faces, we knew we had no choice. The road back to Kanczuga was out of the question.

Fortunately, the river was shallow at that point. I am very small, and, with the heavy pack on my back, the water just grazed the tip of my chin. Luzer was shorter still, but somehow Uncle Sruly managed to hoist both him and his pack onto his shoulders.

It was September, and the rushing water chilled us to the soul. But, somehow, I do not think any of us minded. After the fear we had just felt, we crossed as if making our way to the Promised Land, with determined smiles on our faces and hope in our hearts. I half-expected the San to part for us like the Red Sea.

I do not know how long it took to cross the river, ten, maybe twenty minutes. When we reached the other side, we were so wet and cold and exhausted that we flopped onto the dry ground. No soldiers had stopped us at the shore to hinder or arrest or steal from us. We were free.

Still lying on the grass, I looked up at the sky and breathed my second prayer to God that day: Thank you.

From every direction came whoops and shouts of joy. If we had not been so tired, we could have danced. The worst was over, and we were safe.

Or so we thought.

# Fay

We stayed on the riverbank for perhaps an hour, resting, wringing out our wet clothing and rubbing our flesh to keep warm. A few people gathered sticks and lit fires. Our small group huddled close together, but we talked to everyone. Many of us knew one another, and others whom we had not met personally we knew by sight or reputation. I recognized shoemakers, merchants, tailors, roofers, goldsmiths, photographers, saddlemakers, bicycle repairmen, brickmakers, farmers, even musicians. We could have started our own town here in Przemyśl, on the western bank of the river. All we needed was a rabbi.

I do not know how long we were surrounded by Russian soldiers before I looked up to find them pointing their rifles into our faces, telling us that we were under arrest.

"Sirs," an old man called out in broken Russian. "We were almost killed by the Germans on the other side of the river. Have we crossed from one hell into another?"

The soldiers were unmoved. Perhaps they did not understand him. More likely, they did not care. They rattled off something that sounded harsh and angry. Then they led us to a simple hut, with a flat roof and no windows. There we found other Jews who told us not to worry; we just had to answer some questions, and then we would be released.

"The Russians think we're spies, coming over here to their side of the river," said the old man.

"Why would Jews spy for the Germans?" I asked.

"No, spies for them." He smiled. "But they still want to rough us up a little."

At this, I shook my head. Everybody liked to rough up Jews. From what I had seen in my short life, it was the favorite pastime of the goyim.

"Whatever you do," said the old man, "don't tell them you are

Communists. Communists they arrest right away. They think you expect special treatment and will make trouble."

When we looked at him in confusion, he threw up his hands, as if to say, how should I know what makes these people tick?

The soldiers called people for interviews, while the rest of us stayed behind, reclining on piles of straw on the floor of the hut. I huddled close to my brother. We had no blankets, and our clothing was still wet. I thought I would never fall asleep. But, with all the tension of the day, my eyes were not closed more than a few seconds before I drifted off.

When my brother woke me the next morning, sunlight streamed through the open door of the hut.

"They're interviewing people again!" he said. "I'll bet they'll call us soon!"

My stomach ached with hunger, but all I could think of was how happy I was to see him. When I reached over to hug him, however, he gave me a funny look and shied away.

To hide my hurt, I turned to my uncle. "Uncle Sruly?" I asked tentatively. "Do we have any food?"

He sighed. "Only if you like soggy sandwiches. But don't worry. We'll be out of here soon."

I hoped he was right, but I also hoped I would have a little time to make myself presentable. My long hair was full of straw, and my dress and underwear were damp and wrinkled. I tried to clean myself up as best I could. Just as I was pulling the last few strands of straw from my hair, the soldiers called us out. We were taken to a long, wooden table under the trees.

"What is your name?" my soldier asked me. I did not know Russian, but it is similar enough to Polish that I could make it out.

"Faiga Rosenbluth," I said.

"What does your father do, Miss Faiga Rosenbluth?"

"He is a leather merchant, sir."

"And what is your destination, pretty lady?"

At that I looked into the man's face for the first time. It was softly lined, and his eyes were dark and kind.

I allowed myself a small smile. "I have relatives here in Przemyśl."

"Who are they, and where do they live?"

I gave them Uncle Luzer's name and address. Not until much later did I realize that I could have just as easily lied. But, at that moment, I needed to trust this nice man with the friendly face. I would have told him anything.

After a few more questions, they thanked us politely and sent us on our way. We gathered our belongings, and the six of us set off down the road to town. We were hungry and cold, but, for the second time in two days, we felt that we had cheated death.

We had not gone far when we came upon a small village. Every time we saw a nice-looking house, Luzer would nudge one of the men.

"I think I smell bread baking in this one!" he'd say. "And their cows look like they'd make fine milk."

But Yossi felt that everyone would be knocking on the doors of the homes closest to the river. So we walked on until we reached an isolated hut.

A young woman came to the door, carrying a baby. When she saw us, six Jews looking as if we'd returned from a watery grave, she shrank back and called out to someone in the house. Soon an old man appeared, and the woman stood just behind him, staring at us over his shoulder. Mr. Turm quickly explained that we had crossed the river and were hungry. He said we would pay for any food we would receive. I wondered how he had managed to hold back money from the Germans, but I was too hungry to care.

The old man disappeared into the house, and we sat on the ground to wait. Imagine, I thought. Two days ago, I would not have dreamed of sitting in the dirt like this. How quickly life can change!

Soon the man returned with some meat and bread. He stood over us while we ate, his eyes darting back and forth from our faces to the road.

When Uncle Sruly handed me a piece of bread, he noticed I was shivering. "Grandfather," he said. "The Germans made us cross the river by foot. Do you think we could spend the day in your barn to dry out and press our clothing?"

The old man stroked his chin in thought, then shook his head. "I don't mind Jews," he said, "and you seem like a decent lot. But the Russians are arresting people all over this area. As soon as you're finished, you'd better be on your way."

I said, "But they just let us pass!" The others looked at me in surprise, Luzer most of all. Where I came from, women didn't usually voice opinions in serious matters. Yet somehow, I had the sense that all the rules had changed when we'd crossed the river.

My outspokenness didn't seem to bother the old man. "This is a border area," he said. "It's a dangerous place in wartime."

Wartime. I was so tired of that word! Ever since I'd first heard it, it had turned our lives inside out. At least in Przemyśl, we could be safe until the war was over, which, God willing, would be soon. I was much more worried for my family, left behind under the German occupation.

We set off for the train station, which was a few kilometers' journey. Two young boys offered to help me carry my pack part of the way. I assumed they were the sons or grandsons of the friendly peasant, but I didn't ask questions. I was just glad to be rid of the load.

At last we reached the station. I do not know how long we sat waiting, our teeth chattering and our eyelids heavy, for the train to arrive. At the sound of the engine, the six of us stood up. We found seats together in a corner berth, where we were careful not to look into anyone's eyes or speak any more than we needed to. The last thing we wanted to do was raise suspicion.

Przemyśl boasts a thousand-year history, most of it auspicious. We knew from school that, as the meeting point of the Sandomierska Lowlands and the Carpathian Foothills, it was of vital strategic importance. It had been a fortress city since the eighth century, and the castle had loomed over the town like a watchful caretaker since the Middle Ages. By 1940, Przemyśl was a thriving, cosmopolitan city of shops and factories, parks, and theaters.

When we clambered off the train, I sighed in relief. This seemed like an easy place to be inconspicuous. At that, I had to laugh. Imagine Faiga Rosenbluth wanting to be inconspicuous!

We parted company with our two neighbors, who went off to their own relatives, and headed by foot to the home of my mother's brother Luzer in the Jewish quarter. My Uncle Luzer was a poor man, whose every attempt at business had failed. His apartment was a fourth-floor walk up in a ramshackle building. In a small shop at street level, he operated his own *mangel*, a huge contraption with two big wheels that flattened damp clothing to make it easier to press.

At the sight of that wretched building, I felt the tears well up in my throat. Why couldn't my mother's wealthy cousin Shaye Langsam have taken us in? There we would have had our own rooms. Or he could have opened up the hospital for us, seeing as he was the president. Perhaps it was just as my mother always said. It is not the person who has the most who gives the most.

When he spotted us just outside the door of his shop, Uncle Luzer came around his counter to greet us. He was a dignified little man, with a reddish birthmark on an otherwise angelic-looking face. There was no mistaking the warm smile and the dancing eyes of my mother. He hugged each of us and led us upstairs as if we were the grandest of company and his home the most gracious of palaces. But we were disheveled and dirty, and his two dark, little rooms already housed ten people. My mother had not counted on the fact that another brother and two adult children had come in from Dynów.

As we were warming ourselves by the stove, Yossi asked my uncle about the Langsams.

"*Oi*," said Uncle Luzer, his palm on his forehead as if he were checking himself for fever. "You know they had a wholesale steel business about a block long. A store, a warehouse, the works."

"Had?" Yossi asked, looking up from his cup of tea.

Uncle Luzer nodded. "The Russians emptied everything out, until now it's no better than a big, empty barn. Take from the wealthy; that's their motto. But when will they also give to the poor?"

Uncle Sruly scowled. "And what about the family?"

My mother's brother shrugged. "Gone to Siberia, like everyone else."

Later that day, we gave Uncle Luzer's wife our clothing to wash. Then we crawled under blankets on the kitchen floor, even though it was still light outside.

My brother came in a few minutes after I did. He must have thought I was asleep, because, as he lay down, he stretched out his arm just enough so that our fingers touched. Before, I would have pulled back. But this time, I moved a little closer.

I did not care what time it was, or who stayed up talking and smoking. At that moment, I would have been happy to sleep on that floor for the rest of the war.

# Fay

Each day brought news of Hitler's victories. He had already taken over half of Europe, and his hunger for power and land showed no sign of abating. Thank goodness, the news we got from home was more encouraging. True, they did not know what would be from day to day. But they had enough to eat, they wrote. They had their house and one another. The young people were sent to work for the Germans. But it was not hard physical labor, and, at the end of each day, they returned home.

The Gestapo had ordered the Jews of Kanczuga and other towns across Europe to select a committee to represent them, which they called a Judenrat. Each day, the Judenrat had to determine who was to go to which job, as well as distribute bread and generally take care of administrative details. The committee was even ordered to form a Jewish police squad to carry out its decisions. This was actually something of a relief for the local Jews, my mother explained. At least they were no longer ordered around by the Gestapo or the Polish police.

Most dreaded of all, however, was the fact that the Gestapo had commanded the Judenrat to collect all the Jewish money and valuables, on penalty of death. It all sounded bad, but we didn't care. Luzer and I were homesick, and our uncle and cousin were desperate to see their wives and children. Besides, the apartment was so cramped that, as the saying goes, we had to go out into the hall to change our mind.

Apart from that, we were finding that the Russians were no more trustworthy than the Germans. We had heard that they were dragging refugees from their apartments and sending them to Siberia. Because of this, we slept at someone else's home every few nights. Once, we even hid in Uncle Luzer's store, beneath the mangel, for three nights in a row.

For relief, we started making jokes about the Russians, about how, whenever you talked to them, they always said the same thing: Everything in Russia is bigger; everything is better. And how they bought whatever they could get their hands on, no matter what it was.

In one popular story, a Russian walks into an empty shop and asks the storekeeper if he has anything at all to sell. The storekeeper pulls down some flypaper from the ceiling. The Russian doesn't know what it is, but he buys it anyway and leaves the store happy. Outside, he takes it out, unrolls it and starts licking, thinking it is honey. When his tongue gets stuck, he throws it away, assuming it has gone bad.

Like thousands of others, we decided it was safer to return home. I could already see my mother, standing in the doorway in her apron, the tears streaming down her beautiful face. Of course, I had already seen her that way the day we left for Przemyśl. But, this time, they would be tears of delight.

One night, I was sleeping in the kitchen with the women. My uncle, cousin, and brother had gone off to another town to try to sell some goods. All at once, I heard a loud knocking. Still half asleep and rubbing my eyes, I opened the door. To my astonishment, I found two Russian soldiers pointing rifles.

"What do you want?" I asked.

One of them pulled out a piece of paper from his pocket and unfolded it, in what seemed to me to be agonizing slow motion.

He read out the names in a tired, bored voice. Kneller, Josef. Rosenbluth, Faiga. Rosenbluth, Luzer. Rosenbluth, Sruly.

"Oh," I said, faking a yawn. "They moved out a week ago."

"Well then, you don't mind if we just have a look around, now do you?"

We held our breaths as they tramped around the apartment. When they were gone, we helped the children back to sleep with promises of sweets the next day. More to calm myself than to comfort them, I sang a lullaby I had known all my life.

Belz, mayn shtetele Belz,
Mayn heymele, vu ikh hob
Mayne kindershe yorn farbrakht.
Zayt ir a mol geven in . . .
Belz, mayn shtetele Belz,
In oremen shtibele
Mit ale kinderlekh dort gelakht.

Belz, mayn shtetele Belz,
Mayn heymele vu kh'hob gehat
Di sheyne khaloymes a sakh.

[Belz, my little town, Belz,
My little home, where I spent
My childhood years.
Belz, my little town, Belz,
In the poor little house
Where I laughed with all the children.

Belz, my little town, Belz,
My little home where I had
So many beautiful dreams.]

When the children were asleep, I pulled back the kitchen curtain to peek out onto the street. The sight made me gasp. A family of four was being dragged from the next house and shoved into a truck. Cold with fear, I watched the same scene repeated at the next house and the next, until my aunt gently reached around my shoulder and loosened the curtain from my fingers.

I counted the hours until the others came back. When they did, I rushed breathless into their arms. That day, we started looking for another apartment. No longer did we have any hope of returning home soon.

# Leo

Back in Kanczuga, I'd worked in my father's store since I was a little kid. I was used to working. So, when we got to Przemyśl, I was ready to make a living. But they told us that the Russians wouldn't give refugees jobs like regular people. The only way we could earn our keep was by trading on the black market.

Turns out the black market wasn't a place, like our rynek back home. It was more like a state of mind, where no rules applied except your own *sechel*, or intelligence. We got going the day after we arrived in town. Uncle Luzer gave me a few złotys to get me started. Then I went out onto the street with my uncle Sruly. We split up right away, but Sruly said to keep an eye out for each other in case one of us got into trouble. I had no idea what kind of trouble we could get into, but I thought if I asked too many questions, I'd seem like a dumb little kid. Uncle Sruly was one of those people who knew how to do everything, and I didn't want him to think I was dead weight.

The square was buzzing. Filled with people. It looked a little like the market I remembered from home, except it was very disorganized. People just walked around the crowd, carrying bags full of old clothes, wearing lots of scarves and hats they were trying to sell, holding up a piece of jewelry here, a few spoons over there. I wanted to cover my ears so I wouldn't hear the screaming. Everybody was calling out in these reedy, hungry voices, voices that sounded as if they were about to break with exhaustion and worry.

The crowd was so big that I lost my uncle in no time. At first, I wanted to run back to the apartment; everything was so crazy and strange. But then I noticed that a skinny kid about my age was hawking a man's jacket. I looked it over while he stared at me, as if to memorize every feature of my face in case I took off. The coat was dark wool, a little dirty,

73

but in good shape, with no holes or rips that I could see. I offered the guy fifty złotys, and he took it right away. This made me nervous. I thought he was supposed to bargain to get me to jack my price up. Then I decided that he was just a kid like me and probably didn't know what he was doing any better than I did.

So now I had a dirty jacket, and no more money. This meant it was my turn to circle the market, screaming that I had a "beautiful, warm, well-made" coat for sale. When an old woman offered me forty złotys, I thought I would *plotz*. What if I'd made a bad deal, my first day out? But it wasn't long before somebody gave me seventy, and I was in business.

We'd been in Przemyśl a month or two when the Russians said we couldn't trade on the black market anymore. But we didn't have any choice. It was the only way to make a living. So we watched and we listened, and we avoided the Russian KGB men dressed in plainclothes. It wasn't hard to do. When you're in that line of work, you learn to smell them. We kept our eyes moving, moving over the crowd all the time. Since the police were looking mainly for people trading in gold or dollars, we were pretty safe. But, still, we didn't trust a soul.

One time, a policeman asked whether a pair of pants I was holding was for sale. I knew he was police from his accent and from the way he carried himself so straight in his fake old clothes.

Right away I said, "Oh no, they're mine. I'm just walking around with them because my mother and I are moving, and I have no suitcase."

Or something like that. You wouldn't believe how many people were "just walking around" with shoes, clothing, birdcages—anything they could get their hands on.

Lucky for us, everybody in town went to the black market. The only people who cared whether it was legal were those dumb KGB men, who thought they were fooling us with their terrible disguises.

# Fay

*Oi, oi, oi.* I trudged up the stairs to the apartment we now shared with a widow and her son in another part of the Jewish quarter. Thirty-nine, forty. All these steps were keeping me strong and trim, I told myself, trying, as my mother always did, to put the best face on the situation.

In truth, life was good. We knew how lucky we were. Mr. Turm, who had come over with us from Kanczuga, had been sent to Siberia. But our men spent their days doing business on the black market, selling shirts and scraps of leather out on the street. Luzer was turning out to be an excellent businessman, shrewd and honest at the same time, just like our father. Tata would have been proud of him. I was proud of him.

Although a woman came in the mornings to help with the housework, I was still busy, cooking and sewing and taking care of the men. Never had I been in charge of a household like this before, and it took some getting used to. But the others were grateful for my work and ate whatever I made for them, so I soon stopped complaining and began enjoying all the attention and responsibility.

Best of all, I had just received a letter from Mamche. She wrote that she had sat at the table after we left, missing us and wishing that she hadn't sent us away. And, suddenly, here were two little girls at the door, alone and in a strange place. Who knew where their parents were? Who knew what had happened to them? Someone must have directed them to her, she assumed, someone or something. She offered to keep them, and they were very happy to have a home.

She wrote, I am telling you this because I hope that if you ever need help from a stranger, you will not be refused. I am casting bread upon the waters in the hope that someone will repay the favor to me someday and take in my little ones when they are alone and hungry.

I smiled and folded the letter back into its envelope. I did not expect to have to rely on strangers. We were paying our own way and doing fine. And soon, I was sure, we would return to her.

That night was Shabbos, and, sitting at the table with our landlady and her son, looking into the scrubbed faces of my uncle, cousin, and brother in the velvet candlelight, I was almost happy. Our day-to-day life almost felt normal. All we needed were the people we loved.

Then our landlady said to my uncle, "Did you hear they're sending more refugees to Siberia? From all over the neighborhood?"

My skin got prickly all over. I looked at my uncle. He had been chewing on a drumstick, but now he sat perfectly still, the bone in his hand, the food in his mouth unswallowed.

"Is this true?" he asked. "You are absolutely sure?"

The woman nodded. "They're going from house to house. They have a list of everyone who crossed the river."

I thought of the scene I had witnessed from Uncle Luzer's window and shivered.

"The Russians and their lists!" Cousin Yossi set down his fork with a thump. "I heard the same rumor," he said, "but I didn't want to believe it. What do the Russians have against us?"

Under the table, I reached for my brother's hand. "Does this mean we have to move again?" I asked no one in particular.

No one answered. We ate the rest of the meal in silence, although I, for one, could no longer taste the food. I should have been sad, I suppose, but I wasn't. All I could feel was anger, a fury growing in my chest and threatening to take over my entire body. First the Germans, now the Russians. Why won't they just let us live in peace? We were not murderers or thieves. Our only crime was that we had been born Jewish.

The next evening at the supper table, Yossi put down his napkin and cleared his throat. We all looked up from our plates.

"Here's what I propose," he said. "I will go to Schodnica, stay with my sister a few days, and find us a place to live. Wita's husband, Baruch Fessel, is the son of the chief rabbi. I'll set everything up for us. Then you three can come join me there."

"It's an interesting idea," Uncle Sruly said. "But you've got to be careful."

I said, "But you have no papers! If something happens to you, we will never know!"

Yossi shrugged. "I'll write you a letter," he said. "The Russians are civilized people. Surely they'll let a prisoner write a few lines to his family?" He clapped my brother on the back with a hearty chuckle. But none of the rest of us was laughing.

We were worried about Yossi, but he was adamant. Since Luzer and Sruly were working, I took him to the railroad station. On the walk over, he never stopped talking, even to catch his breath. He described his sister, his brother-in-law, the children. . . . At first, I almost believed that he was simply excited about seeing his family again. But, when he held out a stack of bills at the ticket booth, I saw that his hands were trembling.

When we said goodbye, I hugged him long and hard.

"Goodbye Yossi," I sobbed. "I will miss you so much!"

"Shhh, little one," he said. "We will meet again soon, in Schodnica. You'll see. And when we do, I promise you will no longer have to sleep on the kitchen floor!"

"I don't care if I have to sleep in the outhouse," I said. "As long as you're safe."

At this he gave a hoarse laugh and boarded the train. As it slowly rolled out of the station, he waved his hat, and I watched until it disappeared in a cloud of black smoke.

Two days later, Uncle Sruly sat us down at the kitchen table. "We received a letter today from a secretary for the Russian police," he said with a frown.

At the word "police," I felt an awful clamminess all over my body.

"This man," my uncle murmured, "says a man named Yossi Kneller was taken away as he tried to disembark from a train outside of Schodnica."

He paused, looking up at us over his glasses. Both Luzer and I stared back at him, our faces blank.

"The man says," he continued, "that Mr. Kneller begged him to mail us a letter."

He set down the first piece of paper and plucked a second from the envelope. I noticed his hands were shaking, just like Yossi's at the station.

Yossi wrote, "Dear children, I am being taken away to an unknown destination. You must accept my fate bravely. I hope that I will be the only sacrifice in our family, and I hope the best for all Jews. If you ever meet my family again, tell them for me to be brave."

Luzer sat perfectly still, staring straight ahead. I reached for his hand, and he gave mine a squeeze. Then I ran from the table and threw up in the sink.

# Fay

Yossi's arrest galvanized us in a flurry of activity, all of it motivated by terror. We moved to the non-Jewish part of town, further from the border, in the hope that we would be safer. There we rented a room in the home of an elderly former Supreme Court judge and his wife. The judge was a kind, if eccentric, man who treated everyone with the utmost respect.

Our living quarters were small, and the neighborhood was relatively poor. But, sometimes, I got the chance to walk around the better parts of the beautiful old city, with its wide, tree-lined boulevards, elegant towers, and a concert hall, it seemed, on every street.

Soldiers were everywhere, of course, cuddling on the park benches with gaudily dressed women, strolling through the market, their hands thrust deep in their pockets, or singing songs late at night in booming voices laced with vodka. At first I was afraid, but the judge explained that this was normal in a border town at wartime. Again that word. I felt like screaming whenever I heard it.

"The only reason the soldiers look twice at you is because you're pretty," he said, patting my head. "Don't give them a second thought. They won't hurt you."

At night, I slept in the kitchen, and the men took the bedroom. During the day, while the judge was at court and the men were on the street exchanging their goods for food, I did the washing and the cooking. When the judge came home, he would get very angry with me.

"Why are you working all day long?" he would say, handing me a piece of chocolate he'd bought in town. "You should be dancing!"

"I am lucky just to be alive," I said. I think the answer surprised me more than it did him. When had I become so serious?

But I decided that the judge was right; I should enjoy life a little more.

So I treated myself to a new hairstyle. I had my braids cut off and got a bouncy permanent wave. Immediately I felt older and more sophisticated. Every time I looked in the mirror, I was a little less depressed by this dreadful war.

One day, the judge's wife told me how she had come to marry him. For many years, she had been his capable and faithful housekeeper, managing servants and a beautiful home. Then, when he turned fifty, the judge became very ill. Lying in bed one day, he realized that if he died, his housekeeper would be penniless. Even worse, his snobbish, greedy family would inherit all his wealth. So he married her, right in his sickroom. When he recovered, his family was mortified to have a penniless girl in the family. The judge and his wife, on the other hand, were ecstatic.

It was the nicest story I had heard in a long time. Here were people who were still decent, who knew how to treat others, to look after people in need, even if they had no obligation toward them. Perhaps, I thought, there was hope for us after all.

Then the Russians ordered everyone to take out passports. With our names on their lists for deportation, we did not have a chance. So we wrote to our cousins in Schodnica, who told us that they would help us if we could get to them. It seemed like a good thing to do. After all, Yossi Kneller had risked his life to get there. We just had to be more careful.

Schodnica is nestled deep in the Carpathian Mountains, fifteen kilometers from the closest railroad station. Although several times the size of Kanczuga, it was still a small town, with about five thousand people, a good number of them ethnic Ukrainian. Schodnica was the first place in Eastern Galicia where oil was discovered, thanks to a Jew who was digging a well in his garden. Since then, many Jews had grown wealthy in the oil business and built elegant homes and synagogues.

The Soviets had controlled Schodnica since the start of the war. Almost at once, they confiscated everything the Jews owned, making a thousand people little more than beggars overnight. It was nothing personal, they told them. Being Communists, they simply did not believe in private property.

Somehow we arrived without incident, and Uncle Sruly soon found us an empty store in a building that also housed a beer hall and a factory. He scrounged up two beds, and there we moved our few scraps of clothing, a pot or two, and my photographs from home. Then he and Luzer went out on the street to trade a few things so that we could have something for dinner.

79

I decided to make a cup of tea. But, when I looked around, I realized we had no kitchen. Somebody must have said something to me about it, but I supposed that, in the confusion and upheaval, I hadn't been paying much attention.

I slumped onto one of the beds in despair. Once again, I wondered what I was doing in a strange place, so far away from the people I loved. Nothing, absolutely nothing was turning out as I had planned.

Just then, I heard a knock. I opened the door to an old woman with shadowy eyes and a pale, puckered face.

"Hello, dear, she said. "You must be my new neighbor. Aren't you a pretty little thing?" I nodded, my heart beating a little faster. I thought, Go away, I don't have anything to give you. But I said nothing. Instead, ever so slowly, I began to retreat behind the door.

"Wait," she said, catching the door with her hand. "I live here. We share a kitchen. Come; I'll show you where everything is."

The kitchen was simple, but adequate. As I filled my pot with water, I chided myself for being so suspicious and unfriendly. I thought of my mother, who every day took two pots from our neighbor, Symy Bodek, and heated them on her own stove. Symy lived in a rented room, and even her own daughter wouldn't let her use her kitchen. When my mother would shake her head in bewilderment, I would agree: How could a daughter be so cruel? But, in truth, I had disliked Symy, too. She was hunchbacked and ugly, and I had hated having her around. That day, I wished with all my heart that I had been kinder to her.

Luzer found a job, while Uncle Sruly, who, being past forty years old, couldn't get hired, roamed the streets, doing whatever black-market trade he could. Once again, we settled into a routine. I stayed home and tended to the cooking, cleaning, sewing, and washing, while the men went out into the world. I was often bored, and I missed my family more than I could say. But the sight of those two coming home every evening was a gift that made everything else worthwhile.

Every so often we would receive word from our parents, which was always cause for celebration. Mamche wrote, "Have patience; God is with us. We are well. We only wish we could all be together."

In another letter, she told us that they had taken in a boarder, the woman who used to be the attendant at the *mikvah*, the Jewish ritual baths. The baths were destroyed when the Germans invaded, and so the poor woman had become homeless. Later, Mamche wrote that the woman was ill. Mamche and our neighbor Elka Turm, whose husband had crossed over with us, were up many nights washing and feeding her and changing her linens. I cried over that letter. Certainly my mother was the kindest, most generous person who had ever lived. And what did I have to show for my life?

At night, I slept with those precious pages in my arms. During the day, I carried them in my apron pocket and took them out to read as often as I could. As I pored over each passage, I hoped to find some clue, some new piece of information with every reading. Again and again, the worry would rise to the surface: Maybe we were foolish to leave home. We should have stayed together, whatever happened. Yet, despite our longing for our family, we believed that our best chance for survival was to spend the rest of the war in Schodnica.

We were doing the logical thing, we knew. But logic cannot mend a broken heart.

# Leo

In Schodnica, if a guy didn't work, he was deported. You had to look for a job, then report to a government agency and say you had one, and then the government would let you stay. Yossi's brother-in-law tried to help me find something, but, because I was a stranger, nobody'd take me on. Finally, I bribed the mayor with the little cash I had left and got a job in a woodworking factory. It was in the loft of the same building where we lived. They made wooden wheelbarrows and wagons, that sort of thing.

The foreman, who was also a carpenter, was a Jew in his forties. He was tall, with an honest face, a nice guy you could really talk to. He wasn't well educated or religious, but he was smart all the same. I told him that I'm good with my hands and that I pick things up pretty fast, and we got along fine.

About forty people worked in the place, and they were all good fellows. Because we were in the Russian sector, there were no real bosses. That's the way Communism was. The experienced and talented people just told the others what to do. After I was there a while, they made me in charge of unloading and storing all the wood that came in and checking it to make sure it was what we'd ordered.

I liked being a *macher*, somebody important, and I liked the work. I had always loved making things, and now I was doing it for pay. But I could never just relax and enjoy myself. All the time I was thinking, what will we do if the Germans come?

One day, while the foreman and I were stacking lumber, I stopped what I was doing and folded my arms. After a couple of minutes, he looked at me.

"Well, what is it?" he asked.

"I was just thinking—"

"We don't pay you to think!" he said. His voice was gruff, but he was smiling. Then he said, "So what were you thinking, if I may be so bold to ask?"

I said, "I was thinking that if the Germans take over Schodnica, this lumber is going to last a lot longer than we are. Unless we do something to save ourselves."

He looked thoughtful. "What do you have in mind?" he whispered, glancing around to see whether anybody could hear.

I waited until one of the workmen disappeared around a corner. Then I said, "I was thinking of a hiding place. We could go there if there was any trouble."

He raised his eyebrows. "That's a great idea, but I'm not sure how it would work."

I grinned. "Don't worry. I've made all sorts of things. I know just what to do!"

His eyes gleamed, and he clapped me on the back. "Good boy!" he said. "Let's work on it later today, when everyone's gone."

That evening, we made ourselves a crawl space underneath one of the hundred-foot stacks of lumber. The opening was maybe eight inches high, but, when you slid inside, you could sit up. Nobody knew about it, and they probably would've thought we were crazy if they did. They saw no reason to be afraid of the Soviets who were in charge, and, since Stalin had signed a treaty with Hitler, they weren't afraid of the Germans, either. Why should they be? They hadn't seen what happened when the Germans occupied a town.

Even Jews were supposed to be safe in Schodnica under the Soviets. The Russians weren't anti-Semitic, because everybody was supposed to be equal. They marked "Ivrei" for "Jew" on Russian passports, of course. But I didn't want a Russian passport, anyway, because then they could tell me to go to Russia anytime they wanted or to fight in their stupid army.

When the hiding place was finished, I felt a little safer. Life was okay, except for the first thing in the morning, when I realized where I was, and the last thing at night, when Mamche wasn't there to kiss me good night. But Faiga was so great that she almost made up for it all. We'd bring her food from the black market, and she'd spend all day making soup, beef, chicken, anything she could to make our little room feel more like a home. We were beginning to feel like one person, Faiga and I. I could hardly believe she was the same sister who was always pestering me back in Kanczuga.

Schodnica was a pretty lively town, and the three of us started taking long walks in the evenings. Uncle Sruly would buy us sweets with the few coins he'd managed to pick up during the day. Everywhere you went, you heard Russian music. The soldiers were always singing marching songs. For some reason, if you heard a really nice tune, it made you sad. More than once we'd leave the house chattering, but when we came back later, not a word.

We were in town just a few months when we woke up one night to a blast of gunshots. After the shots was a strange silence. We didn't have a radio, and our neighbors in the building didn't know what was happening, either. But, the next day, we learned that the Germans had invaded the part of Poland that was under Russian control—including Schodnica. So much for their ten-year pact with Stalin! Hitler promised to reach Moscow in three weeks.

He wouldn't succeed, of course, but he did put the Russians on the run. As they left, they destroyed anything they could get their hands on. Then, one night, the oil refinery in Drohobycz exploded with such a terrible thundering that it could've been an earthquake.

And then they were gone. We figured it was only a matter of time before the Germans caught up with us, too.

# Fay

For five days after the Germans invaded, all was quiet, like the terrible stealth of a wolf that is planning to pounce. In the evenings, the tension in our tiny household was so strong that we snapped at one another or kept to ourselves as best we could. During the long afternoons when I was alone, I thought I would go up in flames like the refinery, so fierce and hot were my emotions.

Then the order came that Jews could not be seen on the street without a yellow star. We made them from strips of clothing or material we found in the market. After everything we had been through, they were an indignity, but nothing more. A strip of yellow cloth, we told ourselves, could not break our bones, or even our spirits.

The fourth of July 1941 was a Friday. That evening, I set a frayed white cloth on the table and fit the white candles into our secondhand candlesticks. I was humming one of my mother's favorite songs.

Avinu malkeynu, haneynu vaaneynu.
Ki eyn banu massim.

[Our Father and King, have mercy upon us.
We are unworthy; deal with us kindly.]

Just then Luzer burst into the room. I almost did not recognize him, so distorted were his features. His face was drained of color, and, despite the blistering heat, his teeth were chattering.

I waited for him to speak, but he just stood in the middle of the floor, squeezing and unsqueezing his fists and staring at me, his eyes twice their usual size.

When I took a step toward him, my arms open, he burst into tears and ran to me.

I was ready to cry, too, but I knew he needed me to be calm, so I steeled myself. "Shhh," I said, rubbing his back the way Mamche used to do. "Tell me what happened."

Through his tears, he said, "Oh my God, oh my God! I was out on the street, when suddenly a Gestapo guy turns the corner on a motorcycle at full speed. I ran after him to see where he was going. He went as far as City Hall. Then he went in, but he wasn't there long. He got back on the motorcycle and disappeared."

I was still holding him. "That doesn't necessarily mean anything bad," I said.

He wrinkled his forehead, the way he did when he thought someone did not understand what he was talking about.

"Faiga, they put chains on the Chief Rabbi and attached them to a pair of horses! They're dragging him down the street and beating him with sticks!"

"The Chief Rabbi!" I shouted. "That's Yossi's sister's father-in-law! He must be eighty-five years old! How could they do such a thing?"

I pictured the tall, serious man, who came from one of the wealthiest families in Poland.

"It's more than the rabbi," he said, shaking uncontrollably. "It's every-body! Little kids, they're stabbing and robbing every Jew they see. Old people, young people. Even other kids they go to school with! It's unbe-lievable!"

"What? But that doesn't make any sense! Why would they suddenly start killing us?"

He bit his lip, which was already raw from his nervous habit of chew-ing it. Then he said, "I heard a rumor."

At this, my stomach tightened. Rumors were not always to be be-lieved, but they usually contained some kernel of truth. I released him and dropped into a chair. "What kind of rumor?"

He swallowed hard. Then he said, "I heard a rumor that the Germans have given the townspeople twenty-four hours to do whatever they want to the Jews."

"Whatever they want?" I shrieked. "The *goyim* hate us! They'll rip us to pieces!"

He was circling the table now, and I had to move my head to keep him in my line of sight.

At last he said, "Oh no, what are we going to do about Uncle Sruly? I've got to go find him!"

He was already halfway to the door when I reached him and grabbed his shoulders. I said, "Luzer, listen to me. Uncle Sruly is a grown man; he can take care of himself. We've got to keep you safe. It's time for you to go to your hiding place."

He pushed me away. "Are you crazy! They'll skin him alive! We've got to go find him before it's too late!"

I shook my head. "You know what Mamche told us. You must keep yourself safe to continue the Rosenbluth name, whatever happens to the rest of us. She's counting on you. We're all counting on you. You can't risk your life that way."

I said the words that Mamche would have said, but now they were my words, too. If anything happened to Luzer, I would be devastated.

At that, he grew calmer. "We can't leave Uncle Sruly out there to rot," he said.

"We won't. But you made a promise."

"Yes, but—" He sighed. "You're right. I'd better go."

"Be careful," I whispered.

"But what about you? Are you going to be all right?"

"I'll stay here with our neighbors," I said. "I'll be okay. They usually go after the men in these things. It's you I'm worried about—you and him."

We kissed and held each other close. With my arms around him, I realized how much he had grown since leaving Kanczuga. He was becoming a young man. I thought of how proud my parents would be when they saw him again.

"You know," he said suddenly, "before this, you were always just my big sister, nothing more." He cleared his throat. "You know what I mean?"

When the first tear trailed down my cheek, I brushed it away. I thought of all the pinching, the hitting, the arguments over the years.

"I know," I said. "I also know I wasn't the best sister in the past. But I'll always be here for you."

And then he was gone. The moment he closed the door, I realized that he had forgotten to take along food. I stepped outside to tell him, but he had vanished.

Already I could hear the screams outside. I knew I had done right telling Luzer to hide. But I was as worried about Uncle Sruly as he was. Jews were being stabbed on the street, the most respected of our people was dragged through town by a horse, and I did not have the slightest idea where my beloved uncle might be. Nothing in my life had prepared me for the decision I had just made.

# Leo

My foreman was already in the hiding place when I got there. The boards were staggered in front of us to shut out the light, so we sat in darkness. We didn't dare even to whisper. We heard footsteps walking, then running, maybe four or five feet in front of our faces. Now and then we'd hear these terrible screams, like animals being slaughtered. And because I couldn't see what was happening, I pictured the most horrible things. Then it would get really quiet, and that maybe was even worse.

I thought of my Tata, who had lost his first wife and baby in a pogrom not very different from this. I'd never paid much attention to modern Jewish history, but now I had the feeling I was living it. *Pogrom.* I had heard the word many times but never imagined that I would be caught in the middle of one.

I worried about my sister. Out on the street, it had seemed to me that only the men were in danger, but I could've been wrong. Maybe they started with the men and then went on to the women? Should I have brought Faiga in here, too? I'd kill myself if anything happened to her. I didn't dare think of Uncle Sruly. Whenever I did, I tried to push him out of my head.

I thought about praying, but I had never been the type to daven on my own. It just wasn't in me. If God cared at all about the Jews, he knew what to do without me telling him.

My stomach started to growl. Like a jerk, I had run out of the house so fast that I forgot to bring anything to eat. I found a bit of candy in my pocket, and I gave the foreman half. Sucking on the sweet, I wondered whether I would ever taste food again.

Then, some time later, I realized I wasn't hungry anymore. I wasn't even scared. It's funny. Your mind and body just go numb after a while. I started thinking that whatever will be, will be. Mostly, I thought of my sister, coming to tell us that it was safe to come out again. Faiga, who for me had become like an angel of God.

# Fay

That night, I stayed with our neighbor, her daughter, and her two little granddaughters, not daring to leave the building, but too afraid to stay in our room alone. Our neighbor was a kind, soft-spoken woman, about my mother's age, and when I closed my eyes and listened to her hum over her sewing, I could almost believe that I was home. Not once did she speak about her son, son-in-law, and fifteen-year-old grandson, who were out in town when the massacre began. But I knew her heart was as full of fear as my own. We did not close our eyes until dawn.

In the morning, we were awakened by a terrible commotion. We were so frightened that we did not dare to draw the curtains. Instead, we sat on the bed, huddled together for comfort.

Then we heard a pounding on the door. My neighbor and I exchanged terrified glances. For a brief second, I considered ignoring the noise, but from what Luzer had told me, had we not opened up, the mob would have burned down the building.

I took a deep breath, cast one last look at the old woman, and reached for the knob.

A crowd of peasant women stood at the door. Their blouses were soiled, their eyes murderous in faces dark with sweat.

One of them said, "Step aside, child! We won't hurt you."

"Yeah," said another, pushing her way past me. "We're just doing a little shopping."

My neighbor, who was now standing right behind me, said, "This is not a store! This is a private home."

The mob laughed as if it were a single, fire-breathing dragon, with a dozen arms and legs. The monster poured into the house and sent its tentacles into all the corners, hungry, I supposed, for money and valuables.

One woman said, "No such thing as private homes, when it comes to Jews."

Then someone started to giggle. It was a girl not much younger than I. She said, "Pretty soon, there won't be no such thing as Jews!"

At this the dragon laughed again, ripping out drawers and closets, pawing through the few scraps of clothing and food we had managed to save.

Then someone was pushing us all out into the street. It happened so quickly—silence one moment, these horrible thugs the next—that I did not realize what was happening until we found ourselves outside in the harsh sunlight.

When I turned away from the door, I froze. The street was painted in blood like a gigantic canvas, blood flowing in dazzling rivulets along the pavement, blood running down the faces of young men and suspended, it seemed, in the hot, dank air. All around us people were screaming, women standing paralyzed like us outside their homes, men and young boys falling under the knives and heavy sticks of their neighbors. The noise was horrible. It did not seem human; it sounded like the wild cry of a thousand wounded beasts. But it was so intense that the very earth could have been howling with grief and pain. It was, I thought, the sound of God weeping.

A group of men marched us with the rest of the Jewish women and children to the edge of town. From time to time, a child staggered in the heat; if a woman paused to identify a corpse, one of our guards would hit her with a stick or the heel of his hand or kick her as she struggled to her feet. I walked as swiftly as I could, anxious to find out whether Uncle Sruly—or even Luzer—were among the dead.

Everywhere I looked, the peasants were laughing and swigging vodka, shouting to one another in excitement, admiring each other's handiwork. Small boys with curved knives taller than they were jabbed them into the bellies of their schoolmates and out the other side. Bands of young men pushed doctors and lawyers twice their age in the direction of the woods; for what, I did not dare guess. People tripped over bodies and kicked them aside, as if they were so much debris.

I was dimly aware that I had slowed my pace, unable to march past so much horror. Suddenly, I was being helped up by my neighbor and another woman. I felt dazed and nauseous, and I tasted blood. Somehow the women managed to dislodge us from the group and take me to a nearby house. With each step, my legs buckled under me.

"What happened?" I asked my neighbor, when I felt lucid enough to speak.

She was wiping my head with a damp cloth. "One of them hit you with an iron pipe or something. You passed out."

Another woman I had never seen asked, "How do you feel?"

"My head is throbbing," I said. "But more than that, there's a ringing in my right ear. That must have been the side they hit me on."

"Don't worry," my neighbor said. "That will go away."

I rested in that house for some time. After several more hours, the uproar outside died down, and we were allowed to return to our homes. I did not want to find out what they had done to our belongings, but I wanted to stay out on the street even less.

We went back to our building and slammed the door as if against a hurricane. Inside, the storm had already hit. My neighbor's room was a shambles. Drawers overturned and empty, the bed stripped, the floor black with footprints, pieces of dishes strewn across the few sticks of furniture. She rushed to a little table and turned it over with trembling hands. Then she sank to her knees. They had found her secret hiding place with the few valuables she had managed to save.

I touched her shoulder, but I do not think she knew I was there. Then I trudged over to my own little room. It was the mirror image of hers. Like a mechanical doll in slow motion, I began to pick up the pieces. The cracked mugs, the broken table leg. The feathers ripped from our pillows, a few still floating in the rank air. I worked hard, but I saw nothing. Nothing but the faces of my loved ones.

When I had no more strength, I collapsed on the mattress, now devoid of whatever small bit of stuffing it had once possessed. The food was gone, not that I could have eaten anyway. I was grateful for sleep, but it was a light, restless slumber, full of ghostly noises that may or may not have been real. My ear still buzzed with its strange music, and my head had not stopped hurting since I'd been hit.

The next morning was quiet. At least it's over, I thought. What's done is done. My head felt as though it had been flattened by a tank. I lay on the skimpy mattress, hungry and parched, but unable even to get up for a sip of water.

Later that morning came another pounding outside.

"What more can you take from us?" I cried out weakly. Somehow I managed to drag myself to my feet and open the door, expecting to find another mob.

But this time it was a middle-aged Polish policeman with stooped shoulders and a paunch. He said, "I am under orders to take you women with me to the woods."

I scowled. "For what?"

His pale eyes narrowed a little at my tone. But he simply said, "To bury the dead."

Over his shoulder, I could see a group of blank-eyed Jewish women already lined up behind him, with several menacing-looking officers holding rifles. Instantly I closed the door behind me and fell into place with the others. We marched through the filthy streets like a ragtag army. Most of the bodies had already been removed, but the pavement was stained a reddish brown.

As we traveled through the town, I noticed that the shops were open, and people were going about their lives as usual. Apart from the smashed windows of Jewish stores and the marks on the street, very few remnants of the previous day's massacre remained. It was uncanny that such a tragedy could disappear as though it had never been.

When we reached the woods, many of the women fell to the ground beside the maimed bodies of their husbands and sons. Others stared at a ruined face, trying to determine whether they knew its owner. The place held the heavy stench of death, a fetid, overpowering odor. Some vomited over the corpses we were sent to bury. We found heads smashed in, severed limbs, men hanging from trees. None of it seemed real.

Apart from the names cried out from time to time, we said little. Few of us wept. It was as if we could not allow ourselves the luxury of emotion. We would have plenty of time to grieve later.

Despite my fierce headache, I moved like a madwoman, trying to catch a glimpse of every corpse in the hope of locating my uncle. Or, more accurately, in the hope of not finding him at all. As the terrible day wore on, I began to believe that he had survived. If Luzer had managed to hide himself, why not Sruly? He was such a determined man and always so certain that everything would turn out all right.

We were ordered to dig graves. When someone asked for a shovel, the policemen laughed.

One of them held out his meaty hands. "These are your shovels!" he said. "Now, get to work!"

I looked at my tiny, pale fingers, the nails pink and clean, the white half moons roundly even. My hands were made for embroidery and crochet, for drying tears from a baby's cheek.

"You there, what are you waiting for? Your Messiah?"

At the sound of the ugly laughter, I fell to my knees and sank my hands into the earth. The first touch of the rich Polish soil calmed me, somehow. If I tried very hard, I could almost believe that I was back in Kanczuga planting vegetables. True, I hadn't liked getting my hands dirty even then. But, compared to the hell in which I now found myself, my short foray into gardening was a heaven I would gladly have returned to.

An older woman worked alongside me. She had a pinched, yellow face, and her lips never stopped twitching, as if she were lost in prayer. Her movements were quick and intense, like those of a dog digging up a bone. At first I tried to match her pace, but I soon grew tired and short of breath. Besides, we weren't dogs, and I had no wish to become one. Luckily, the policeman didn't watch us too closely.

When we started, I wondered what we would do when the graves got too deep for us to stand in. But I soon found that we were expected to dig wide and shallow holes, like the footprints of elephants.

At dusk, we were sent back to our homes. Not daring to go out to Luzer, I stayed in the apartment, listening to the death knell in my head and staring out the window at the empty, blood-streaked street. What would I do if neither one of them had survived? How would I have the strength to live? I could not imagine it. Instead, I waited. When I could no longer bear to watch for them, I lay in bed, my eyes open in the dark, my ears pricked to the slightest sound of a key in the lock, a scratch of pebbles on the windowpane.

# Fay

On the third day, I took Luzer what little food I could gather together from our neighbors. The factory itself was a disaster, but the little fortress was still intact. Holding my breath, I knocked on the panel that I knew to be the entranceway. When I heard his answering knock and then saw his face, I let out a whoop of joy.

"Shhh!" he said. "You want to give us away now?"

He was scowling, but his eyes were merry. I could tell he was pleased to see me.

"It's over," I said. "Everything is quiet again."

He sighed. "Let's hope so. How bad was it? Are there any men left?"

When I said nothing, he shut his eyes. After a few seconds he said, "Did you hear anything from Uncle Sruly?"

I shook my head. "But they sent the women out to bury the dead, and I looked at every body. He wasn't there."

He said something, but I could not hear.

"What did you say?" I asked him.

He looked at me curiously. "Thank God!"

"Oh. Of course. Are you ready to come home?"

He ducked back into the enclosure, and I heard him speaking to his coworker. When he returned, he said, "We're going to wait a little longer. It'll be dangerous for us out on the street, with all the Jewish men gone." He sighed. Then he said, "You know, we're going to have to get out of Schodnica."

"As soon as we find him," I said.

"Yeah." He reached down and hugged me tightly. Despite my fear, I was pleased.

Then he noticed the bandage. "What happened to your head?"

"I was hit."

He pursed his lips. "Are you okay?"

"I think so."

Once more he sighed. It sounded like the lament of a man three times his age. He said, "You'd better go now."

We hugged again, and then I left.

The next day, my neighbor knocked on the door, calling my name. It was afternoon, but I had been sleeping on and off, trying to dispel my dizziness.

I jumped up and opened the door at once. "I heard some news," she said.

"News about my uncle?"

She nodded, her face grim. Without a word, she led me back to the bed.

My head was still throbbing, and the incessant ringing was driving me a little crazy. I said, "Tell me what happened to him."

"My child," she said, taking my hand. "They found him in the woods, near the water, with a bullet in his shoulder."

I did not dare to breathe. "Only one bullet in his shoulder?"

I thought of all the torment, the terrible destruction of bodies I'd seen in the forest. I asked, "Then he's all right?"

She looked down at her hands. They were swollen and red, the nails bitten halfway to the cuticles.

"He was probably afraid to come back to town. He must have crawled to the water to get a drink. And that's where he bled to death."

Despite all the corpses and all the blood, I could not take it in.

"My uncle is dead? From a wound in the shoulder?"

"Blood, my dear. He lost too much blood. He was lying there for two or three days."

Perhaps it was because of my head wound, my fatigue, or something else, but I needed her to repeat the story. When she was finished, I said numbly, "So he's dead. Now there's only Luzer and me."

We sat holding hands, without speaking. The room had begun to spin, and the sounds in my head were mocking me.

After a while, she asked, "Do you want to come back to my room tonight?"

I shook my head. She had lost her son, her son-in-law, and her grandson. It was unfair to expect her to comfort me. Besides, all I wanted to do was stay in bed.

I said, "There is nowhere to go to get away from it anymore. Wherever I am, I take it with me."

After she left, I lay in bed staring up at the ceiling, thinking of my own impotence. I wanted to cry, but I had no tears left. I wanted to scream, but I could not summon the strength. I wanted to die, but my brother needed me. Most of all, I wanted to be in my mother's arms.

When Luzer returned home later that day, I told him everything that had happened. He did not speak. He simply surveyed our little room with dismay. We had no food, no clothing, and only each other to rely on. Our neighbors were happy to help us, but they had nothing, either.

We decided to go out to the woods to forage for food. It was the same place where I had dug the graves a few days earlier. But the horrid smell was gone, and we avoided the low mounds of dirt. With my brother beside me, I was not as frightened.

"You know," he said, bending down to pick some mushrooms, "there's nothing keeping us here now. I can't work. I can't even trade on the black market. And since the Germans are here now, too, we might as well go home."

I stood still, holding a sheaf of grass in my hands. "Of course!" I said. "There's no reason not to!"

At this, my heart lightened. I did not even mind eating the sour grass and mushrooms that night. We were going home!

The next day, we hugged our neighbors goodbye. They had been so wonderful to us that we could hardly bear to leave them. The old woman wanted to give me something to remember her by. First she reached for her finger, but her rings had already been taken. Then she stood up and pulled out a drawer, but it was empty. Despite our distress, we laughed at her attempts to find something, anything to give us. At last, she reached for a small stone she had used to mash mushrooms.

"Take this," she said, "and remember us. We love you and wish you well."

We had nothing much to carry. That evening, we walked to Borysław, the nearest town. Then, we got a lift with a peasant to Drohobycz, where a distant cousin gave us a place to sleep for the night. Somehow, I had managed to hold onto my gold earrings, and I sold them so we had a little money to live on. From town to town we hitchhiked, until we came to Sambor.

In Sambor, we could catch no more rides, and Jews were not allowed to travel by train without a permit. So there we stopped, in a strange place, not knowing a single soul, with winter fast approaching. We were hungry and cold, as lonely and desperate as we had ever been. Our only consolation was that we had each other.

# Leo

I don't know how long we stood out on the street after our last ride dropped us off. The cold air stung my cheeks and nose. I kept pinching them, thinking that would keep them from freezing. My eyes were wet, too, and I tried to shield them from the wind by ducking into a doorway.

Then it hit me that it wasn't the wind that was causing my tears. That made me mad. I was sixteen, long past my bar mitzvah. I was supposed to be a man. Some parts of being a man I'd handled just fine, like getting us rides all the way to Sambor. But finding us a place to live? The idea made me shiver. Or maybe it was just the cold.

I looked at my sister. The wound on her head was an oozing welt. She was biting the nail of her left pinky. She was crying, too. But she was also looking around at all the people and signs and cars, as if she didn't even notice the tears. It was as if crying had become so natural that we didn't even think about it anymore. Sort of like breathing.

I wondered what I would think of Faiga if I were seeing her for the first time. By me she was a pretty girl, long brown hair that could've used a comb, small but strong, nice clothes that'd seen better days. I wouldn't have thought she was twenty-one, though. As she wiped her nose with the heel of her hand, she looked like a scared little kid who'd got lost in the big city.

A car went by real slow, looking for a place to park. I caught a look at the driver. About my father's age, he was. But this guy was as different from Tata as you could imagine. Fat, with a round face, no beard, and bald as a chicken's egg. He was talking very fast to a woman at his side. She was blond and painted like a movie star.

I turned back to Faiga. "So what do you think we should do?" I asked.
"What?"

I'd noticed lately that she was having trouble hearing me. I didn't want to say anything to her about it, though. I just repeated the question.

She shrugged. "What can we do? We don't know a soul."

"Well, we can't stand here."

"You know," she said, shaking her head, "this is so unfair. All the times people came to Kanczuga without money or food, with no place to stay, and our parents took them in. Why, on Shabbos, Tata actually had to scour the town for a beggar before Mamche would give him his own supper!"

"I know, Faiga," I said. "I was there with him."

"So where is Sambor's Itczy Rosenbluth to come and take us home with him?" she wailed. "Are we going to end up as beggars in the street?"

Then she looked up at the sky. "It's getting dark," she said. "What are we going to do?"

She was going on pretty loud. People were staring at us, but she didn't seem to notice. Everything we did seemed like it was happening to somebody else. Or in a dream.

I tried to think. What would Uncle Sruly do? But the thought of our uncle made me so sad that I just wanted to curl up in one of those storefronts and bawl like a baby.

"Okay," I said. I reached for her hand to calm her down, but she shook me off.

"Why don't we find someplace that's open all night, where we can get out of the cold?"

At that, she nodded and almost smiled.

"Like the train station," I said.

But then right away I shook my head. No, no good. If Jews aren't allowed on trains, why would they let us hang around a train station?

"I know!" she said all of a sudden, her eyes lighting up. "I know! I know where we can find Tata in Sambor!"

For a second, I thought that the fear and cold had gotten to her. I said, "Faiga, relax."

"No, I'm serious! Where does Tata find beggars?"

I shrugged. "In Kanczuga! Nu? What good does that do us?"

She held my hands and danced me around in a half-circle. Instead of staring at us, people on the street now made a big point of looking the other way.

"The shul! We'll go to the Jewish quarter. I'm sure they'll help us!"

The answer was so simple that I laughed. I said, "Great! Let's find out where it is, quick! I'm freezing!"

Soon we were in a dirty neighborhood of peeling storefronts and pot-holes. It was way past dark, and Faiga and I linked arms to keep warm. Before we got very far, a man came up to us. He had a blue star of David on a white armband on his black coat, a long, brown beard, and a gray face.

"Hello," he said. "You children from around here?"

All we did was tell him our story, and he was taking us home with him. He lived in a shabby, two-room basement apartment that was full up with kids. Jews weren't allowed much coal to heat their stoves, but it was still warmer than it was outside. His wife gave us steaming tea and small wedges of salted bread.

"Rosenbluth, eh?" the man said, scratching his cheek as he watched us devour our food. "I know a widow name of Rosenbluth. You got any relatives in Sambor?"

"No, sir," Faiga said. "I'm sure our parents would have told us if we had."

He shrugged. "Well, no harm in asking if she'll take you in for a while. You can see for yourself we don't have much room for you here."

The next day, the man walked us the few blocks to the widow's house.

It had two rooms, but the widow lived only in one of them. It was a cramped little place that was always bitter cold. The windows were so frosty that we couldn't even see out.

In the other room was a shoemaker and his wife, who was blind. Be-cause they weren't Jewish, they could get plenty of coal. Sometimes they let us come over to warm up.

The days passed slowly, like water running uphill. The Judenrat as-signed us work to do for the Germans. Seems that they always sent me to the worst places with the heaviest lifting or the messiest jobs. I couldn't blame them, really. They wanted to take care of their own people and didn't care so much about strangers.

So there I was, working ten-to-twelve-hour days loading coal on trains, on Shabbos yet. My parents would've been furious, but I didn't mind, as long as I was taking care of Faiga. The thing is, no matter how much I worked, I had nothing to show for it. I went out every day in below-zero weather in a torn shirt and smock. Finally, the Judenrat gave me old boots and a coat. The boots weren't even a pair; one was two sizes bigger than the other. Sure, the coat had a fur collar. But it was probably older than I was.

The first time Faiga saw me in that get-up, she broke into tears. I teased her that she would cry at anything, but, when I imagined what I looked like in her eyes, I was ashamed. And for the first time, I was thankful that my parents and friends weren't there to see me.

Our stomachs never stopped growling. Month after month, we had no milk, no butter, and about half a slice of bread a day. At home, we lived on a thin gruel that Faiga made by throwing a little wheat in a coffee grinder. She cooked it with saccharin and water. The only thing that saved us from starving was the soup kitchen, where Faiga went every day to pick up our supper.

My sister wrote home, telling them that we lived with a nice woman, but that we were starving and cold. Actually, I'm sure she put it better than that, because she didn't want to worry them too much. But we were hoping they would get the point.

One night, I dragged myself home from work as usual, so tired I wasn't even hungry. All I wanted was to fall into bed. As I reached our house, I saw Faiga's eye in the little hole she always made in the frost to watch for me.

She opened the door when I was still pretty far away and motioned for me to hurry. It was all I could do to walk, much less run. But I was freezing, so I managed to sort of trot the last few steps.

"You'll never guess; you'll never guess what I have for you!" she said, clapping her hands in delight.

Something was different about the house, but I was too worn out to think what it was. I nodded hello to our landlady and sat down at the table. My teeth chattering, I took the hot cup of tea Faiga handed me.

"A package from home, I hope," I said.

My sister looked a little disappointed, but just a little. She said, "You guessed it! A peasant came this morning with clothes, money, and a letter!"

"Thank God," I said. "What does the letter say? I'm too tired to read it myself."

"It says that they are very happy to hear from us and that they're all well. Things are tense there, but they've got plenty of food, and they're even doing a little business now and then."

"That's great," I said, draining my cup. "Now, I've got to lie down. I feel really lousy."

She pouted, just a little, but it was there. "What about your supper?"

I waved her off. "Take it. You can give me your soup tomorrow; how's that?"

101

Then I realized what was different about the house. The smell. I hadn't smelled anything like it for what seemed like years.

"What—what did you make?" I asked.

She took my hand and led me over to the oven. When she opened the door, I gasped. It was the biggest goose I'd seen in my life!

"Have you changed your mind about dinner?" she asked with a sly grin. "Or do you still want to take a nap?"

I pinched her, like the old days, but gently this time. If I'd been a little cleaner, I would have kissed her.

"I'll be right there," I said. "Let me just wash up a little."

"This should last us a couple of days," she said. "No soup kitchen for a while, huh?"

A few minutes later, the widow and I sat at the table, and Faiga brought the roasted goose on a big plate. We mumbled the blessing before food. I was so hungry that I didn't wait for her to carve it; I just ripped off a drumstick and gnawed at it like an animal. Nobody said a word. I guess I should have been embarrassed, but with hunger there's no place for embarrassment.

I chewed the bone until every scrap of meat was gone. Then I licked the juice off my fingers. Then I took another piece.

In half an hour, the goose was gone. So much for no soup kitchen.

# Fay

Throughout much of Europe, the winter of February 1942 was one of the fiercest on record. We gained some small comfort, at least, from the knowledge that the Nazis were suffering on the Russian front just as we were in Sambor. Their troops got as far as Stalingrad and could go no further. It was their first setback, and we were thrilled. Thousands of German soldiers froze to death in the icy forests, but we had no pity for them. As far as we were concerned, it was too few.

I spent the icy days keeping our room tidy and doing some sewing and cooking, but my main occupation was worrying. I worried mainly about my brother, who was working too hard and eating too little. When I tried to give him my bread in the mornings, he always insisted that I eat it instead. We were both pale and undernourished, but I did not care about myself. I was determined to get him home safely.

I was sure that one of the German "actions" would occur any day, which meant that my brother and I would be rounded up and deported to a prison camp, if not simply killed outright. Just as the Judenrat had chosen him for the worst jobs, they were sure to select us for a Nazi transport if it meant protecting one of their own.

One evening, we were sitting at supper when we heard a knock on the door. We looked at each other in panic. Who would visit us at this time of night?

My brother motioned to keep quiet and tiptoed to the window. He put his eye to the hole in the frost that I had made earlier that day while awaiting his arrival. Our landlady and I held our breaths.

Suddenly, Luzer let out a hoot so loud we both jumped. He reached the door and tugged it open in one quick motion.

I gasped. It was two of my dear friend Bruchcia's brothers, Sany and

Chaim. I ran to them so fast that, despite my small size, I almost knocked them down.

"Is that the way they taught you to greet visitors in Kanczuga?" Sany laughed. "Some upbringing you must have had!"

For the rest of the evening, we sat around the table laughing and talking. They both looked so thin that I ached to feed them, but all we had to share was our hunger. Every so often I reached out and stroked their hands or faces. They looked at me a little funny, but I think they understood. They carried with them a small piece of Bruchcia, a piece of our lost life.

Our friends had crossed the San about the time that we did, and now they were making their way back home. Like us, they were afraid to get caught in an action. Also like us, they had no one to look out for them and nowhere to hide. They had made the decision to leave just a day before doing so. Bruchcia was going to follow them a little later.

Listening to them that night, it seemed to me that we had only one option: to go home. We knew from their letters that my parents were still in our house and that, apart from one action, which had scared them terribly, they were living with little fear. The problem was that moving from town to town as a Jew without a permit meant certain death. We could not even apply for one, because we had gone to the Russian sector, so we were labeled Communists. The Germans would not only shoot us if they found out; they would shoot our parents, as well.

Day after day, lying on my little mattress, I turned over the possibilities in my mind. At last, I narrowed them to one. We had to take off our Jewish armbands, go home by train, and live in hiding.

It was too dangerous for us to go to the train station to purchase a ticket, so we hired some Gentiles to do it for us. In case an action came in the next week, we decided that Luzer should go first.

My parents sent another Gentile couple from Kanczuga to accompany Luzer on the trip. I could not go with them to the station, of course, but we stood just inside the door to our house and hugged as though we'd never see each other again. That was the thing about war. You never really knew if you would.

He tried to be brave, but I could see him shaking. I thought of Yossi Kneller, and I held him all the tighter.

"Be good," I said. "Get out of here before it's too late. And give Mamche a kiss for me!"

I watched him from the cleared space in the frosty window until he was out of sight. My head buzzed as if it were full of bees.

Our landlady was sitting at the table drinking tea. I think she asked me if I was all right, but I couldn't quite make out the words. I nodded and lay down on my mattress, my face to the wall.

The next week passed so slowly, I thought I would never live to see the end of it. Every day, I went about my few chores and collapsed on my mattress as quickly as I could, hoping to sleep away the time. But, at last, the day of my departure arrived. I dressed in peasant's clothing: a colorful kerchief, a loose blouse, and a long skirt. I hugged the widow and thanked her for her kindness. Then I opened that door for the last time. A gust of wind hit me so hard that I took a step back, then started again.

As I walked to the station, I could feel my heart in my chest, thumping like a cavalry unit. The station was filled with people carrying what looked like all their worldly belongings. Soldiers were everywhere, laughing and clapping each other on the back. I decided that the crowd was a good thing; people would pay less attention to me. I also decided that if anyone spoke to me, I would pretend that I was mute. My Polish was more than fair, but I did not want any slip-ups to give me away.

When I entered the train, it was even more crowded than the station had been, and I didn't see any seats. The car was a steamroom, and I was afraid I would faint from the heat. Then an old man lifted his bundle and motioned for me to sit next to him. I hesitated. What if he were to start a conversation? But I quickly realized that I would be more conspicuous if I were to refuse the seat. So I nodded my thanks and sat down.

I closed my eyes and pretended to sleep. In truth, I had never been so alert in my life. Every sound of a door sliding open, every chance remark filtered through the humming in my brain. Some of the words were muffled a bit, but still I listened carefully.

All at once, I was hit by the full force of what I was about to do, and, despite the awful heat, I started to shiver. I had left home with Luzer, Yossi, and Sruly. Now, I would have to face those two families and explain why my brother and I had survived, while their loved ones had not. The thing was, I had no idea why. Nothing I knew helped me understand the reason for what had happened to my beloved cousin and uncle. With my eyes closed, I saw Yossi shaking at the station. I saw all those bodies in the forest in Schodnica. I knew these were pictures that would be in my head forever.

The ride to Przemyśl took several hours. Not once did I look out the window. I did not dare move, even when I felt the old man nudge my shoulder when someone came by selling cakes. All I wanted to do was disappear. For a few seconds, I almost regretted going home.

But when I reached the station at Przemyśl, my heart lifted. I was so close! For a fleeting instant, I considered stopping by my uncle Luzer's place to see whether he was all right. But I immediately realized the folly of that thought. I would be lucky just to make it home; there was no point in tempting fate. And I was so anxious to see my family that putting it off another few hours made no sense at all.

At last, I alighted at the Kanczuga station. I gazed at the little station house, the train tracks, the platform. None of it had changed from a year and a half earlier. I looked at the area where my friends and I used to fox-trot on Shabbos afternoons in another lifetime. Funny, I could barely remember doing it anymore.

Then I lifted my little bundle, took a deep breath, and set out on the short walk home.

# Leo

Walking from the station into Kanczuga, I spotted some of my father's customers. It was so weird. They saw me all right, but no one said hello. Just before I turned the corner to the Ulica Kolejova, I came across one Jew, with a big yellow star on his coat. He was scurrying along like a mouse, his eyes on his feet, obviously anxious to get where he was going and off the streets as fast as possible.

When I came to our store, I fought hard to control my feelings. They were so strong, and suddenly I felt so weak. It was a weekday, but the place was closed. The big plate-glass windows were dusty, with snow piled a yard high against the stone walls. I opened the door and went through to my family's house. The first person I laid eyes on was Tunia. At least I guessed it was Tunia. When we'd left, she was six, and now she was eight. She had our mother's big gray eyes, and her expression as she lifted her head from her knitting was as sharp and dark as her clacking needles.

She looked like she was about to scream, so I blurted out, "Tunia, it's me, Luzer! I'm home!"

Then she let out a squeal and rushed into my arms. Senia must've heard us from the other room, because she came in, too. What a beauty she'd turned into! Her face lit up when she saw me. We hugged, and I kissed them, over and over. Then they were both talking at the same time, telling me stuff like how, since they still couldn't go to school, they were getting pretty good at knitting and crocheting.

My back was to the kitchen door, so when the girls stood real still, I didn't know why. Then I wheeled around, and there stood my mother. My first thought was how bad she looked. Her eyes were shadowy, and her nose was red, as if she had a cold. Her mouth was more pinched than I'd remembered, and her hair was grayer.

At first, neither of us moved. What could we say or do that could make up for all the time I'd been gone? But that didn't last long. In a couple of seconds, we were in each other's arms. She tried to speak, but she was crying so hard, I couldn't catch a word. No matter. Standing in her arms, I shut my eyes and ears and just hugged her. She felt bonier than I'd remembered, smaller all around. But, for the first time in about a year and a half, I was just where I belonged.

One of the children ran to get Tata, who'd been lying down. When he came staggering out, still drowsy from sleep, I almost plotzed. His payos were gone, just like mine. So was his beard. But, worst of all, his eyes were hollow and colorless, as if they'd been plucked out or something. I would never have picked him out in a crowd.

That week, the whole family, cousins and everybody, sat together trading stories and laughing and crying. I told them about Yossi and Sruly, cursing my luck at getting home before Faiga. Everyone went silent, and the wives and children left the room. But, in fact, it went better than I'd expected. Even my mother recovered much faster than I'd expected. That was the newest thing about my family. They had heard every story and were prepared for every tragedy. Nothing shocked them anymore

The family was different in another way, too. Senia, always obedient and sweet, now did the housework if my mother was sick, which was happening more and more. My parents had tried to hide her with a farmer months before, but he had thrown her out the next day, after stealing everything she had, even her earrings. Someone had spotted her tramping through a field, soaking wet in a country downpour. Since then, I was told, she had become quieter and not so trusting.

But, mostly, life wasn't much different at all. Good old Rózia Kwasniak came at night to help out, even though it was forbidden for goyim to work for Jews. Seeing her heating laundry in a big pot and hanging it in the freezing garden to dry just as she'd always done made it easier to believe that nothing important had changed.

Faiga came home a week after I did. I was so glad to see her that I held her until she finally pulled herself away, laughing that she couldn't breathe. I did it because I'd missed her, but I knew it made Mamche glad to see how close we were. The only thing that bothered Mamche was Faiga's hair. She'd gotten a permanent wave in Przemyśl, and Mamche told her that in the middle of all the suffering it was frivolous to get such a fancy hairstyle. Still, everybody thought it looked nice.

With all of us together during those long winter nights, it was almost as if the war had never happened. And when we sat around drinking tea and Faiga's girlfriends came by and we laughed and talked till midnight, we could make believe that everything would be okay.

We had enough money, and in the basement we still had plenty of potatoes, apples, pickled sauerkraut, and other food to last us a long time. For safety, we had to stay off the streets, but even that wasn't so bad. Tata spent most of his time in study and prayer. In a way, you would have thought he'd have been in Paradise, because that was what he liked to do best. But on his face, in the stoop of his back and the curve of his cheeks, you could see how he really felt.

Mamche tried to stay cheerful. She baked special kugels and still sang from time to time, although her voice wasn't what it used to be. Only at night, the sound of her weeping tore us from sleep like an alarm.

Every day brought more news of disaster. Shootings and deportations. New restrictions on Jewish activity. Our mayor did what he could, but he didn't have any real power anymore.

But none of it mattered, really. The six months after we returned home were the best of our lives. I think maybe we all knew, deep down, that the end was near, so we enjoyed every minute we had together. Faiga and I weren't allowed to leave the house, because no one apart from our closest friends could know that we'd come back. But apart from that, it was like a Shabbos that never ended, together every minute with the people we loved best in the world.

Then, one day, we heard that some people who, like us, had returned from the Russian side, had been shot in their homes by the Gestapo. It had happened in another town, but still we were afraid. Mamche rushed Faiga and me to a woman whose son had been sent to a concentration camp. Our mother brought food for us every night. Since the woman was alone anyway, she was happy to have us.

This went on for several weeks, until one night, Mamche didn't come. We didn't know what to do. All night, Faiga paced, not saying a word.

Next morning, Mamche showed up, her eyes swollen. She said she had heard that the Gestapo was looking for people who had returned from the Russian side. She had been afraid to come to us in case she was followed.

My sister got hysterical. "I am through leaving you," she sobbed. "I can't do it anymore. I can be happy only when I'm near you."

We followed Mamche home. The next day, I started to build a hiding place in the attic. I made a second wall about two feet in front of the first.

Two of the boards were removable, so I could climb in there at the first sign of danger.

Then we were told that Hitler had ordered mass executions and the liquidation of all the Jewish neighborhoods. Nobody wanted to talk about it, but nobody could talk about anything else, either.

One night, we heard a knock on the door. We all looked at each other in terror. Then a soft voice called out in Yiddish. Tata opened the door at once. It was my aunt's brother, but he looked like a madman. He was dressed in rags, his eyes were wild, and his hands never stopped moving. He was the only survivor from his town, he said. The Gestapo had marched the Jewish population to the cemetery. When he got there, he saw a huge pit, with the upturned earth to one side, soaked in blood. Inside the pit he saw the naked corpses of his neighbors. Their clothes and belongings were neatly folded in piles a few yards away.

The man stuttered when he talked, all the time keeping his eyes on the floor.

"I knew I had n-n-nothing to l-lose," he said. "So I just t-turned to one side and ran. They f-f-fired at me, but they missed."

Mamche said, "And they didn't run after you?"

The man shrugged. "W-w-why should they?" he asked. "Th-th-they know as well as I that there's n-no p-p-p-place to hide."

For a long time, we all stared at him in silence. Nobody knew what to say.

Things moved quickly. First, we had to register. Little did we know that our signatures signed our death warrants and made our bankers our beneficiaries. Then we were given registration cards in different colors. We were told they were for work. How we wanted to believe it!

That night, we held up our cards at the supper table. Everybody's was green except Tata's. His was yellow. Yellow, we knew, was no good.

Mamche shook her head. "What will become of you when we go to the work camp?" she asked.

He held up his hands. "What's the difference?" he asked. "Do you really think it makes any difference at this point?"

Faiga said, "You can have my card, Tata. We won't need them anyway."

"Don't say that!" Mamche said sharply. "Faiga, I want you to go to the Judenrat tomorrow and see what you can do to change your father's card."

Even if my sister could've done something, it was too late. We were ordered to report to the main square on one of those miserable July days

110

when the sun beats down as if it has it in for you. When we got there, the square was crowded with people from all the nearby villages. I thought of how we used to dress in our best clothes to stand in that same square with our teachers on national holidays. The band would play Polish songs, and our mayor would come out to greet us.

This time, there was no band and no mayor. Just a Gestapo man making a speech, telling us to come back in a week to be deported.

Fay at age 13, 1933. On the back of the photograph is written "Balci's girl," in Yiddish.

Tunia Rosenbluth, Fay and Leo's youngest sister, mid-1930s.

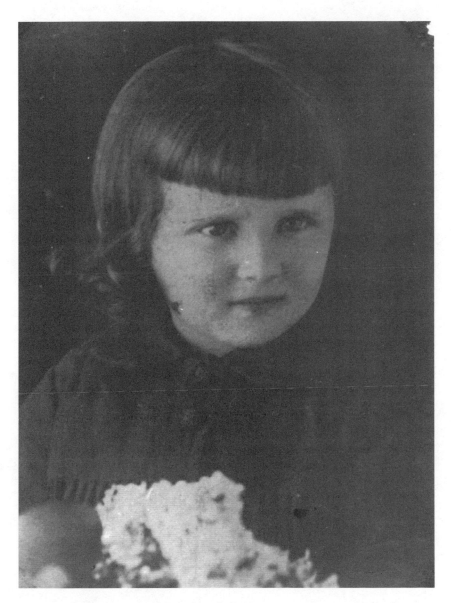

Senia Rosenbluth, Fay and Leo's sister, mid-1930s.

Fay and her closest friends in Kanczuga, 1936. Bottom row *(from left):* Gittel Maber, Runia Feingold, Malka Kramberg, Chajka Shiffman. Top row: Genendla Westreich, Fay, Bruchcia Laufer. Missing is Faiga Ziegman.

Kanczuga boys: Hersh Ziegman *(top)*, Motti Langsam *(center)*, and
Mr. Dombusz, first name unknown *(right)*, 1937. The fourth boy is unknown.

Fay's Russian identity papers photo, 1940.

Fay and Leo's mother, Balci Rosenbluth, 1941. Fay's friend
Bruchcia Laufer was the photographer.

The Skoczylas family, 1950.

Andzia gave this photograph of herself to Leo when he left the
barn to return to Kanczuga in 1944. On the back are the words,
"If you remember, keep it. If you forget, throw it away."

Leo, on returning to Kanczuga after leaving the
Chmuras' barn, 1944.

Mayer Langsam, 1944. Written in Polish on the back of this photograph are the words "I'm sorry I didn't tell you."

Fay's wedding, 1945. Fay is standing in white with a white hat; Joseph is to Fay's left and behind her. Leo is kneeling at bottom right.

Fay and Joseph Walker en route to the United States, 1947.

Leo's wedding to Ethel Biglaiser, 1952.

Leo's three sons *(from left)* Ira, Barry, and David, at Barry's bar mitzvah, 1974. The woman lighting the candle is Andzia Chmura.

Benny Shanzer (Yankele Kelstecher) and his wife, Margaret, with friends, 1990.

Leo and Fay in Brooklyn, New York, in the early 1970s.

# Fay

Now every day was market day in Kanczuga, but the only commodity bought and sold was Jews. Gentiles streamed in from the countryside eager to make a deal. This one would hide your son for so-and-so-many złotys, to keep him from being sent to a labor camp. This one would hide your baby girls and grandmother so that they would not be shot.

Many families made such arrangements for their loved ones. Others set out for other villages and open spaces just hours after the decree was issued. But the next day, the heavens poured down their fury, and people hiding with their small children in the fields had to make their way back to town, drenched and frightened, into the hands of the Polish police.

We also planned to live out the war in hiding. Our Tata, master businessman and Talmudic sage, an ordained rabbi who had translated the entire Passover Haggadah into Yiddish, arranged it carefully. He gave gold and silver and a sewing machine to a wealthy farmer named Zajac, with the understanding that when the time came, he would do what he could for us.

Over the past months, Mamche had grown gaunt with worry. One morning during that last, terrible week, she spun through the house like a wounded bird, fighting to fly. My brother and I watched her silently, at once trying to stay as close to her as possible and to keep out of her way. The little ones nibbled on sweets and busied themselves with sewing. Sewing, I thought, watching their small fingers skip across the colorful fabric. What a gesture of hope! But despite the make-work, once or twice during the day, Senia broke down in tears from the tension. As for Tata, he moved between the desolate house and the empty store like a ghost, speaking to no one, not quite focusing on our faces when we managed to capture his attention.

Then, one day, Mamche stood still in the middle of the kitchen floor, put her hands on her hips, and said, "Luzer, Faiga, get yourselves dressed. Pack a few things to take with you."

I caught my brother's eye. His look seemed to say, Why just us? I shrugged, but said nothing. For once in my life, I was determined to do exactly what my mother asked without argument or annoyance. Besides, what was the point of arguing? Instead, I concentrated on what to pack for this second journey. I thought back to our preparations for leaving for Schodnica two years earlier. Without warning, my dead uncle's face appeared before me. To dispel the image, I moved like a film in fast forward, as if to avoid having to watch myself, to piece together the reality of what was happening. I threw together a few changes of clothing, a couple of pictures of my family and friends, and wrapped them together in a large scarf.

As soon as I tightened the knot, I tore it back open and pulled out the photos. I leafed through them until I stopped at a shot of Bruchcia and Runia in the Laufers' garden. Bruchcia had stuck a daisy in her hair and held another in her hands; both wore the flowers in the buttonholes of their coats. My beloved Bruchcia appeared to be rising from the flowers, a flower herself, smiled upon by the sun. Or, instead of flowers, with their waist-length hair and dazzling smiles, my two friends could have been fairy princesses, or angels come to earth for a short visit.

"Children, quickly!" Mamche was already at the door, adjusting the *sheydel* she wore to cover her hair, when I tiptoed into the empty store to say goodbye to Tata. He was sitting on a high stool at the counter, staring straight ahead. He hugged me, but I cannot say for sure if the event registered in his brain.

Mamche hurried us along the empty streets and shaded country roads. Dust sprayed our pretty shoes like powdered sugar. On the way, we spoke very little. I remember her hard breathing, her mouth set in a determined line, her head held high.

We moved along the dirt roads at a fast clip, but, as if in a dream, we seemed to make no progress. Sometimes a poor farmer with a horse and wagon passed us by, looking through us as if we were invisible. Nobody spoke to us. Nobody looked in our direction. We could have been part of the scenery, like the stalks of corn in the fields, standing pale and unbending in the harsh sunlight.

The day was hot and humid under a cloudless, azure sky, perfect for lazing in the garden under the trees. What was I doing here? I should be sitting at our garden table, sipping cold tea. I should be lying face-down with Bruchcia on her bed, our feet up in the air, gossiping about boys. I should be anywhere but running for my life. Inside, I screamed, fighting for air. *This is not my life!*

I glanced over at my brother. To my amazement, his expression was perfectly normal and calm, as if we were merely rushing to an appointment. Was it possible that he felt nothing, that he didn't know what was happening? Or perhaps the feelings roiling within me didn't show on my face, either. Perhaps I looked like the pampered daughter of a wealthy man, dressed in my good coat and high heels, on my way to a country dance? At the thought, I almost smiled. My mother, dragging us along to a country dance? Not if I lived to be one hundred and twenty.

At last we arrived at the home of a shoemaker in the village of Nizonticze, perhaps a five-mile walk from our house. Mamche banged on the primitive wooden door with the heel of her hand. When the man appeared, they exchanged a few words, while my brother and I stood discreetly to one side, just out of earshot. I had this sense that I should try to appear as mild-mannered and attractive as possible, but my heart was not in it. I did not feel up to selling myself, even to save my life. I watched my brother give halfhearted chase to a couple of chickens pecking around in the yard. They were so helpless and foolish, I wanted to cry.

Then, too soon, the door creaked shut. We looked up; Mamche was still facing the cottage, her hands in fists at her sides. I wondered what she had offered the shoemaker to take us, what he had refused in order to save his own skin.

Our mother did not meet our eyes when she turned away from the door, and not once did she appear to notice us on the hike back into Kanczuga. At one point, my brother reached for her hand, but she ignored him. I imagined that she was scrolling down her mental list of customers for a place to hide us. Who was honest, who was greedy? Who only pretended to be interested in our family? Who had ever made an appreciative remark about the Nazis?

When we returned home, I flung myself onto the bed, dropping my bundle on the floor beside me. The room was cool and dim, a welcome respite from the late summer afternoon. I rubbed my cheek against the sweet-smelling pillowcase. I don't know how long I lay there, or when I fell asleep.

Suddenly, I felt my mother's hand on my back.

131

"Taigale," she whispered, smoothing my hair. "Another shoemaker has promised to take you. Koval."

My heart caught in my throat at the sound of her voice after so much silence. "I know Koval," I said. "He's a good man. His son Błażek has always been nice to me."

"By me, Koval is a *tzaddik*," she replied, "a righteous man. He will save your life."

I rolled over on my back and took her hands in mine. For an instant I was shocked at how she had aged. In my exhaustion, I had momentarily expected the bubbly, energetic Mamche of two years earlier, but this was an old woman, tired and frail.

"What about Luzer and the rest of you?" I asked.

"We will go to Zajac, as planned. It's better this way, if we're not in the same place. Just in case."

Her voice trailed off, and for the second time that day, I had a sense of unreality, as if we were all playing parts in a play.

I sat up, and we held each other close for several minutes.

"I want," she whispered, "that you should be a good mother to your children. A loving wife to your husband."

My eyes filled. "Of course, Mamche."

"I have taught you to raise a Jewish family. To keep a kosher household."

"Yes, Mamche," I said, swallowing.

"You are a good girl, and I am very proud of you. If I could give Hitler my body to save yours, you know I would do that."

"I know."

She took my face in her hands. "I hope you can forgive me, Faigale."

I was startled. "For what?" I asked. "What could you ever have done that needs forgiveness?"

"If it hadn't been for me, you would have been in Palestine by now."

"Oh, Mamche. Don't think of that."

"It's true. You were right; I was wrong. Can you ever forgive me?"

In response, I kissed her cheek.

Then she said, "There's something I didn't tell you, something that happened while you were away. I didn't want to worry you at the time."

I sat bolt upright, unable to imagine what gross indignity she had been made to suffer. "What happened?"

She sighed heavily. "One day, a boy from Kanczuga came back from the

132

Russian side. I went over to ask if he had seen my children over there. He said that he saw your brother all the time, but that he had never seen you."

She shivered, and I held her tighter.

"I got so worried that I couldn't stop crying. I became very ill."

"Oh, Mamche!" I said. "And the doctor isn't allowed to treat Jews anymore! What did you do?"

"He finally came anyway, the Jew-hating momzer. I gave him a lot of jewelry. And you know our doctor. He loves money even more than he hates Jews."

"Thank God!"

"Anyway," she said, "your friends were very good to me. They came over every day. They even slept here sometimes, although I was contagious."

She hesitated. "I didn't tell you that story for your sympathy, you know. I told it because I want you to know how much I love you and worry about you."

"I know," I said, feeling the tears wash over my cheeks. "I know you do."

I pulled myself to my feet and went to look for my brother. When I found him in the garden, I wrapped my arms around him.

"Be good," I said. "Don't give Mamche and Tata any trouble."

He shrugged. "Of course I'll be good."

I realized that I had said the wrong thing. My brother was already a young man, with the faint hairs of a moustache above his lip and a wavering pitch to his voice. Rather than be good, we needed him to be strong. We needed him to take care of our family.

Then I said, "You know, I love you a lot, Luzer."

He took a deep breath, then let it out slowly. "I love you, too," he said. "Don't worry. We'll see each other again soon."

I set off by foot and reached Koval's house by nightfall, weary and thirsty. He took me to his barn and showed me, almost apologetically, a corner of the floor where I could hide among the straw.

"We'll be building you a better hiding place, of course," he said.

For my part, I behaved as if he were the concierge of the best hotel in Kraków. For a "tip," I gave him my gold watch. He thanked me profusely and disappeared back into the house as fast as he could. I did not mind. All I wanted to do was sleep, for the rest of the war, if at all possible. I remembered the last time I had felt that way, back in Uncle Luzer's apartment in Przemyśl.

For two or three days, I lay in the barn, sleeping, daydreaming about the future, doing anything I could not to think of what had become of my family. I was not uncomfortable, and Mr. Koval's two sons brought me food and water and stopped to chat whenever they had the chance. We talked about the war, about whether or not the Americans would rescue Poland. We gossiped about some of the people we knew. Błażek, the older one, asked me why I hadn't gone to more dances, and I explained about my religious parents.

Then, on the third day, Koval himself appeared. He stood just inside the door, as if afraid to come any closer.

"What's the matter?" I asked, my chest tightening. "Is it my family?"

"I don't know about your family," he said slowly. "I just know about my own."

"What do you mean?"

"I can't keep you here, Faiga. I'm sorry. It's too dangerous for us."

"But Mr. Koval!"

"I'm sorry," he said again, staring down at his boots. "That's my final word. You will have to leave tonight."

"But—?" I stopped myself. He had already made his decision.

"I'm sorry," he said for the third time. "Please leave us tonight. Błażek will bring you something for your journey."

Soon after Koval left, Błażek appeared with a bundle of food. He sat down beside me and took my hand.

"I'm very sorry to see you go, Faiga," he said.

"I wish your father felt the same way."

"You don't understand," he said, shaking his head. "My father is a good man. But Kwasniak has poisoned his mind."

I felt a burning in my stomach. "Kwasniak? Our handyman?"

He nodded. "He came to see my father and told him he was crazy to risk his life for a Jew."

The room started to spin. I steadied myself against the barn door and closed my eyes. The ringing in my ears grew louder.

"My parents were going to give the Kwasniaks our home and store when they left," I said at last. "He must not want us to return."

Błażek frowned. "That explains it. Greedy bastard. Anyway, where do you want to go? How can I help you?"

I opened my eyes, looked into his. They were as warm and as blue as the summer sky. "There's only one place I can go. Back to my family. They're hidden with Zajac. Will you take me there tonight?"

"Of course," he said. "I'll come back for you after supper."

When he reached the door, I called out to him, and he turned back.

"I'll never forget you as long as I live," I said.

He smiled. "Then I hope you'll be remembering me for a long, long time."

# Leo

A few pieces of clothing and jewelry, that was all we packed. Then, after dark, the five of us left Kanczuga, leaving the keys to the house and the store with the Kwasniaks. We didn't tell them when we'd be back, or whether our property was a loan or a gift. What was there to say? They waved goodbye, as if we were going on vacation.

Mr. Zajac lived in a village called Siedlecka, a few miles outside town. He had a pretty good-sized house, with an old barn set back from the road.

Right away we knew something was wrong. The man rubbed his hands and wouldn't meet my father's eyes. His wife muttered something to him in Polish behind her hand, and I caught the word for Jew: *żyd*.

At last Zaja said, "I think you've been followed. Do you know Chmura, the farmer?" My father nodded. "I'm going to take you over there. Just until we know it's safe."

Even a Talmudic scholar can't argue with that kind of logic when his family's life is at stake. We followed the farmer down the village road to Mr. Chmura's house. No one said a word. Mamche held Tunia in her arms, which she hadn't done for years. My little sister was snoring softly, as if she were home in bed.

When we got to Chmura's, we said goodbye to Zajac. I turned and watched him grow smaller and smaller as he retraced his steps back to his home.

I knew Mr. Chmura from the store. He was a good man, well over six feet, blond and handsome, a lot older than my father. He'd been in America for a while before the war and had opened a little manufacturing business with the money he'd made there.

I waited outside with Mamche and Tunia. We looked up at the stars, while Tata went in to explain what was what. He came out a little later

136

and led us to the barn. By now, it was very late. No one complained when we bedded down in straw that smelled of animals. Snuggled alongside Mamche, the little girls were asleep in seconds.

Just as I was dropping off, I heard voices. Tata jumped up, straining to hear. The sound grew louder, then soft again.

Tata was just turning to sit down when we heard a knock on the barn door. Mr. Chmura appeared and motioned for him to follow. In the lantern light, I saw his eyes were wide and sad.

They were gone a long time. Mamche and I didn't dare say a word, but we couldn't fall asleep, either. I wanted to go out to pee, but Mamche motioned to me to wait. She buried her face in the straw so I wouldn't hear her cry.

Finally, Tata returned. "What is it?" we asked. "What happened?"

We had no lantern now, so I couldn't make out my father's face. He waited a while before speaking. When he did, his voice sounded as if he were a hundred years old.

"Chmura here says that Zajac will not take us back."

"What?"

"There's more. Kwasniak told Zajac he would be a fool to keep us even one night. So that's what Zajac told Chmura. That the police will come and burn down his house."

"Momzer!"

"Yes, but Mr. Chmura is a good man. A religious man. He cried when he told me we have to go. But he has eight children. He can't risk them for us."

"What are we going to do, Itczy?" Mamche asked.

By now Senia was awake, rubbing her eyes and holding my mother for all she was worth. I wished I were small enough to do the same.

"He agreed to take one of us," Tata said. "Senia can pass for a little Polish child. She will stay here. The rest of us will go back to town."

My sister sobbed and clung to my tiny mother so tightly she looked like she would break her in two.

"Never! Never will I leave you!"

My mother didn't argue. "Then, Luzele, my son, it is up to you."

"Why me? I don't want to, either. I don't want to stay in this stinky old barn!"

"Don't argue with me, mein nachusl. For you, there is no choice. You are our only son. You must stay alive to carry on the family name."

My heart sank to the ground, but I knew the talking was done. Tata went out to tell Mr. Chmura that I would stay with him. When he returned, it was already dawn, and he began his morning prayers. Senia was snuffling in her sleep, curled beside Tunia. I told my father that I would pray later.

But I wondered whether I would ever pray again. I lay close to Mamche in the scratchy hay, like I was a little kid again. Somehow, she still smelled like cinnamon and sugar, the scent of my childhood. Every few minutes one of us slapped an insect off our skin.

At one point, she began to sing to me. So faint, her voice was. Like she was already far away.

> In dem beys-hamikdesh, in a vinkl-kheyder,
> Zitst di almone Bas-Tsiyon aleyn.
> Ir ben-yokhidl, Yidelen vigt zi keseyder
> Un zingt im tsum shlofn a lidele sheyn:
>
> Ay-lyu-lyu-lyu . . .
>
> "Unter Yideles vigele
> Shteyt a klor-vays tsigele,
> Dos tsigele iz geforn handlen—
> Dos vet zayn dayn baruf:
> Rozhinkes mit mandlen;
> Shlof zhe, Yidele, shlof.
>
> Es vet kumen a tsayt fun ayznbanen,
> Zey veln farfleytsn a halbe velt;
> Ayzerne vegn vestu oysshpanen
> Un vest in dem oykh fardinen fil gelt."
>
> Ay-lyu-lyu-lyu . . .
>
> [In a corner of the Temple
> The widowed daughter of Zion sits,
> Rocking her only son Yidele to sleep.
> She sings a tender lullaby:
>
> "Under Yidele's cradle
> Stands a snow-white kid.
> The kid has been to market.
> That will be Yidele's calling, too—
> Trading in raisins and almonds.

138

So sleep now,
Yidele, sleep.

"There will come a time
When railroads will cover half the earth
And you, too, will earn great wealth.
But even when you are rich, Yidele,
Remember your mother's lullaby."]

Too soon it was dawn, and we were saying our goodbyes. I shook hands with my father. Then I hugged my sisters, giving them each a little pinch on the arm for luck. As for Mamche, I clung to her like I was drowning, and she was the last bit of dry land in the world. Tears poured down our faces, blending together into a salty stream.

"My son," she whispered. "I hope that you are in the right place, and that you will live to see the end of the war. Remember, you are a Jewish child. If you meet Faiga, I hope that she too will live according to God's will. Marry Jewish wives and husbands, and tell your children what happened to us. We are doing God's will. If He spares you, tell the world what Hitler did to us."

I couldn't believe what was happening. As she turned to go, I grabbed hold of her arm.

"No!" I shouted, so loudly that she put a shaking hand over my mouth. More quietly, I added, "If you're going to die, I want to die with you. I can't live without you, Mamche!"

"You are going to live to tell them," she whispered. "You are going to live to tell them all the truth of what happened here. Please, my son, do this for me."

I let go of her then. Never have I done a harder thing.

Just as they were leaving, Willy Gross, a boy I know from school who must have been hiding nearby, approached Tata.

"Where are you going, Mr. Rosenbluth?" he asked.

"We really don't know. Back to town, I suppose."

"Mind if I go with you, then?"

I found out later that Zajac had watched from his yard to be sure that we all left Chmura's barn. He counted: One, two, three, four . . . five. Then he returned to his house, shutting the door with a satisfied thump.

139

# Fay

Błażek and I waited until late that night, when every window was dark. Then we slipped past the main road and headed for the fields, so as to avoid the police. When we reached Zajac 's house, Błażek stayed by the road to act as lookout, while I knocked on the bedroom window.

A minute or so later, Mr. Zajac opened the window. The moment he caught sight of me, he hung his head. I had not gotten two words out when he was explaining to me that keeping my family would have put him in too much danger.

"But I thought you had made a deal?"

He hung his head. "Yes, but then I had a talk with Kwasniak—"

I was seething by this time, but I held my tongue.

"Don't worry, my child," Mr. Zajac said softly. "Your family is in a good place. They're with Chmura, and everyone knows that he is a saint."

I thanked him and trudged back to Błażek.

"Well?" he asked, when we had returned to the fields.

Good as Błażek was to me, I no longer felt safe telling him where my family had gone. What was more, I was suddenly afraid to risk my family's lives by showing up at any house where they were hiding.

I said, "My parents left yesterday, but Mr. Zajac doesn't know where they went." Błażek offered his condolences. We talked for a few more minutes, but finally he turned and headed home. What more, after all, could he do for me? We said goodbye in a field, where I bedded down as best I could among the rows of corn.

I lay awake all night, hopelessly awaiting the dawn. What for, I had no idea. I could not go back home. I could not go to my family, and I had no idea when I would ever see them again. Hitler had won victory after victory, taking over Austria, the Sudetenland, Bohemia, Moravia, and now Poland. His Nazis considered themselves masters of the world. And, for all intents and purposes, that is exactly what they were.

# Leo

I lay in the dark for hours. It had to be daylight outside, but in my hiding place, cut off by the slanting roof and removable boards, it was the dead of night. I couldn't sit up. I couldn't cough. I couldn't move.

The thing was, I didn't even want to. Maybe I was in shock, or close to it, anyway. Plenty of terrible things had happened to me in the past year, but nothing had prepared me for this. I was buried alive, and, what was worse, I kept thinking about my family out there. God only knew where.

Mr. Chmura had asthma. He told me that he would go outside his house and cough to let me know he was coming into the barn. That way I wouldn't get scared when the door creaked open late at night.

When I heard him come in, I peeled apart the boards that hid me and hopped down into the hayloft. I hadn't realized that my right foot had fallen asleep, and I almost broke my neck when I landed on it and it gave way.

"Be careful, there," he said, hanging his lantern on a nail on the wall and setting down a tray of food beside me. "We don't want you to do yourself in—"

I could guess what part of the sentence he'd left out. *Before the Germans do.*

"So how are you doing?" he asked, trying his best, I thought, to sound like we were just two guys having a casual chat.

"Not too bad," I said, rubbing my foot, which had gone from numb to pins-and-needles.

The food smelled great, and I realized for the first time how hungry I was. But I had something more important to do first. My muscles were so cramped that I couldn't sit still. Instead, I stretched.

"Good idea," he said, settling down on a bundle of hay to watch me. "You want to keep in shape."

"Oh, it feels so good!" I said, cracking my shoulders.

141

I must have been talking a little too loud—unless it was the crack of my bones—because Mr. Chmura shushed me immediately.

"My wife and three of my children know about you," he said, "but the others do not. They're too young to keep a secret. And, of course, my deaf-mute boy Tolek—he doesn't even know what a secret is. If he found out about you, you'd be entertaining half the neighborhood in here. He has a way of getting into things. And although he can't speak, he does make some pretty loud and strange noises, especially when he gets excited."

"Sorry," I whispered. "I didn't know."

I started to run in place, as quietly as I could.

"Don't worry about it," he said. "Just don't forget it." Then he looked down at the food. "Aren't you hungry?"

"Oh, I'm starved!" I didn't want him to think I was ungrateful, so I stopped running and shoveled down the bread and potatoes and chicken as quickly as I could. I was eating so fast that I didn't even think until I was halfway through the meal that this was the first treyf I'd eaten in my life. Non-kosher food at last, and I hadn't even noticed! Everything was so strange, it was just part of the nightmare.

As I was sopping up the last bits of gravy with a crust of bread, he said, "I'm sorry about your parents, you know."

I nodded.

"I mean it. I lay awake the whole night, praying for guidance."

"Mr. Chmura," I said, "your responsibility is to your family. My father's is to his. That's just the way it is."

He reached out to tousle my hair. "You're a fine boy. I'll take good care of you."

We talked a little more, then he told me he had to get back to the house. As he reached for the lantern, he asked, "Is there anything I can get you to make you more comfortable?"

"I just wish I had some light. It's hard to lay in the dark for so long."

He bit his lip. "I can't give you a lantern. It would be too dangerous."

I could feel my voice getting more excited, so I tried to keep it down.

"I wouldn't need a lantern," I said. "Just a tiny pinhole in the ceiling, so I could see during the day. I could make one with a nail."

At that, he reached up to the wall and knocked off the nail where he'd just hung the lantern. He handed it to me.

"Thanks a lot!" I said. "That should do it."

He smiled. "Just keep the hole small. And tomorrow, I'll bring you a

142

newspaper so you can read up there. That way maybe you'll be able to keep from going crazy."

I grinned. "That would be great!"

He watched while I climbed back into the cubbyhole and folded the boards over myself. Once more I was shut up in darkness.

When he called out a whispered "God bless," I tapped on the boards in response.

I didn't notice till he was gone that I hadn't even said the blessing before the meal. Should you say it for treyf? I wasn't sure.

# Fay

The fields sparkled before me, doused in sunshine. It was late summer, not yet harvest time. Birds twittered greetings among the trees, and the air was rich with the scent of growing things. I passed many peasants on their way to work, hoes and shovels slung across their broad shoulders.

I had a story to tell and a new name to hide behind. But lots of people seemed to know me from the store, even if I did not know them. People kept stopping to tell me that I should hide myself, that the police were picking up Jews all over the countryside. I was heartened and amazed by their concern.

While they had plenty of advice, however, the peasants were short on invitations. And without someone to hide me, where could I go?

Yet, despite my desperate situation, I could not help humming to myself. I was young, attractive, and walking down a pretty country road on a glorious summer day. I knew the noose was tightening around me and my family. But the rope was invisible, and that day I had trouble believing it existed at all. Life was too beautiful. I had been raised to love it, and that was a hard habit to lose.

After a time, I came upon a little spring. Kneeling down to take a drink, I gazed into my shimmering reflection in the water and studied my features. I did not look particularly Jewish, I decided. And my Polish was good, even if I never had been able to get the hang of pronouncing my R's. I leaned back a little to catch the total package. Although my hair was fixed simply, I wore a fashionable two-piece dress, with matching high heels. Hmm. Maybe I was not as pretty as my mother said, but I certainly had a nice way about me.

Back on the road, however, I began to notice that all the passersby were barefoot. The women wore wide skirts, loose blouses, and kerchiefs, the men torn pants and shirts. Be practical, Faiga, I chided myself. How long do you think you can last in these fancy shoes? And this expensive dress? Anyone seeing me in this outfit would know that I did not belong here. I stood out just as if I had two heads.

My stomach growled. I looked up at the sun, straight above my head. It was noontime, and I had eaten no breakfast. In my pocket were just fifty złotys. Nevertheless, I was determined to get something to eat.

I came to an isolated house a good distance off the main road. My feet were already sore from walking, and I was eager to take off my shoes and sit down. I knocked, but no one answered, so I walked in and looked around. The floor was bare earth, and there was a table near the window, a few chairs, and a wooden bench.

Glancing outside, I caught sight of a middle-aged woman leaving the barn with a big pitcher in her arms. I could smell the fresh milk from where I stood, and the scent made me feel faint with hunger.

When the woman opened the door, she was so surprised that she nearly dropped the pitcher. Before I could open my mouth, she said, "Jesus Maria, aren't you afraid to walk around like this? Last night on that hill, I saw a whole family shot down! You know them, from the textile store. The Pinelises."

Now it was my turn to be startled. "You know me?"

"Of course! My whole family used to buy from your store. You don't remember Dudek?"

The name sounded vaguely familiar, but it didn't matter. Mrs. Dudek's friendly words washed over me like a loving embrace. Maybe, I thought, she would want to help.

But my relief was short-lived. The wooden door creaked open again, and in walked a man, slightly older than Mrs. Dudek, with narrow shoulders, a thicket of silver hair, and a mouth sagging with worry. He did not look like the sort of man who would want to put himself at risk for anyone, especially a Jew.

The man had started to say something to his wife when he noticed me from the corner of his eye. He looked me over from head to foot and nodded, as if he too knew who I was.

"So, you have a visitor?" he said to his wife, still looking at me. He continued, "Maciej just came from town. He had no words to describe what's going on there."

145

He paused, and I held my breath. He seemed friendly enough, but I already knew from experience that that did not mean a thing. What was he going to do?

Suddenly he said to his wife, "Give her something to eat and put her in the attic. It's too dangerous for her outside."

My cheeks burned with pleasure and apprehension. They were going to help me, although why, I had no idea. Maybe it was a trap? Maybe they figured I had some money tucked away, and they planned to take it and kill me?

Of course I had no way of knowing, and I had no choice but to trust them.

I gave them what little money I had, and they led me to the attic. It was dark and rimmed with cobwebs, and I noticed a few rotten boards that I had to avoid for fear of falling through. But, otherwise, it was as good a hiding place as I could hope for. Maybe, I thought, they will let me live out the war here. I could certainly do worse. I just had to come up with some way to repay them for their kindness. And fast.

Every day, Mrs. Dudek brought me food and news of Kanczuga. The younger and stronger Jews were being sent to a munitions factory in Stalowa Wola, but, so far, my family had not been touched. Neither had my friend Bruchcia's family, she told me, in answer to my queries. Bruchcia was one of her husband's regular customers in the market, and he knew her well.

That gave me an idea. I told Mr. Dudek to give a message to Bruchcia when she came to buy fruit from him. The next time he saw her, he told her that I was in his house.

Bruchcia knew just what to do. She went home and returned to the market an hour later with money and clothing. Now I could pay Mr. Dudek. But I had enough for only a couple of weeks. After that, I would have to think of something else.

Meanwhile, the deportations were progressing at full speed. Sometimes, the Nazis did not even bother with transport. Anyone who refused to obey the police was shot on the spot, and the corpses were disposed of by Polish workers.

Each day I asked for news of my family, and each day I was told that, although Jews were being picked up all over, so far they were safe. I knew it was only a matter of a week or two until my question would be answered differently. In the meantime, I prayed for a miracle.

146

# Leo

Was it morning? I had no idea. I figured I'd slept some since Mr. C.'s last visit, but how much I didn't know. You might think that sleep would've been a nice break from the boredom of lying here. But it didn't work that way. Instead of flying free in dreams, I just wallowed in the muck. And, when I woke up from these dreams, from seeing the faces of Yossi and Sruly and that wretched sole survivor from his town, I felt worse than ever. If such a thing was possible.

While I slept, I clutched the nail in my hands so I wouldn't drop it and have to wait another day for sunlight. Now, here it was in my palm, sharp and compact and sturdy as could be. Was it time yet? Was the cement roof thin enough to make this work? Again, no idea. Slowly at first, then faster and faster as I got more excited, I began to scratch, scratch on the ceiling above my head. Plaster flaked into my eyes and mouth, but so what? As I worked, I held my breath, till the job seemed more like a frantic struggle for air than a hopeful attempt to find light.

When the sun suddenly streamed in, I gasped. It was a feeling like— like I'd struck oil or something. How to explain how important something as simple as light can be when it's been gone? I held up my hand to the goldenness of it, blocking it and unblocking it, teasing myself with how easy it was to lose it again. I watched the play of light on my fingers, then on my belly. I really wanted to stick my eye in that old hole, to soak up as much sunshine in my brain as I could. But since I couldn't sit up, I had to be satisfied with enjoying it from a foot away. I measured the hole with my fingers. It was a little smaller than when I linked my thumb and forefinger together. It was a beautiful hole. The light pouring through— it was a golden string connecting me to the world.

That night, Mr. Chmura brought me the newspaper. I must have thanked him for that nail a hundred times. I made such a fuss that he crawled up to look at it himself, to feel how big it was, in case it could drown his barn during a rainstorm. I think he got a little spooked, up there in my hiding place. When he jumped down, he had this look of pity that chilled me.

Instead of the nail, the newspaper lay in my hands that night. It was like Chanukah, so excited I was for morning. Except, of course, that Jewish holidays start at sunset. At dawn, I spread the paper out on my stomach, eager to catch the first rays against the headlines. Reading on my back, through that string of light, was tough; I could see only one word at a time. But I managed. And, when I read what was going on outside those walls, I sure wasn't going to complain.

# Fay

By day, I crouched in the hot, dank attic, pinching my feet to keep them awake while I peeked through a crack in the wall at the life below. That crack became my radio and my stage play. It was the only thing that kept me feeling the least bit human.

From dawn to well past nightfall, people came and went in the little house, laughing and trading stories. I grew to like and respect these humble peasants. They worked hard and enjoyed every minute of their rest.

As endless as the days were, the nights were even longer. I had too much time to think and too much time to cry.

One evening, Mrs. Dudek brought me a simple meal, as usual. But, instead of sitting to talk, she immediately turned to leave.

I was too startled to call her back or ask what was wrong. Besides, I wasn't well enough acquainted with her to know what to say.

She had almost closed the passageway to the attic when she opened it again and climbed back up. I looked at her curiously, a piece of bread in my hand.

Her lips were set in a straight line. At last she said in a low monotone, "I have something to tell you. Something very sad. Your family is dead."

I opened my mouth, but no sound came out.

She continued, "They rounded them up, they took all the Jews, and shot them in the Jewish cemetery. The men first. Then the women and the children."

Again, I tried to speak. Nothing. Not a sob, not a word.

I watched a single tear slide down her ruddy face. "Do you understand?" she asked, reaching over to shake my shoulder. "Do you hear what I am saying?"

I nodded.

Mrs. Dudek shook her head, crossed herself, and patted me on the shoulder. "I am sorry for you, dear girl," she said. "You are an orphan now."

When she turned to go a second time, I opened my mouth once more, willing myself to speak. I think I would have clawed the words out of my throat had they not come.

I must have made some sort of noise, because she stopped and faced me.

"What did you say?" she asked, her eyes wide.

"My brother," I whispered. "Was my brother with them? Was it my parents, the little girls, and my brother, too?"

The seconds between the question and answer could have filled a thousand years.

"You know," she said, screwing up her eyes, "I don't think I heard anything about the boy." Then she frowned. "Such pretty little girls."

"Could you," I asked in a hoarse whisper, "could you find out if my brother is alive?"

"Of course," she said. "I'll ask Dudek to talk to them in the market. He will tell you tomorrow."

That night, I stayed up long past the time they went to sleep. I lacked the light to look at my few snapshots, but I tried to conjure up my beloved family's faces in the dark. The only one whose features came into view with any clarity, who wasn't swathed in shadows, was my brother.

My brother had to be alive. I concentrated on that. It was all I had.

# Leo

I wasn't hiding in Mr. Chmura's barn long when I met his daughter Andzia. She was about my age, and she had to be just about the most beautiful girl in the whole world.

Andzia was the first girl I ever really got to know. I'd talked about girls with some of my friends, not the religious ones, of course. But we didn't have classes with the girls, so we didn't have much chance to spend time with them. Except for our sisters and cousins, but then they don't count.

Andzia had long blond hair like sprays of gold; she was tall, with the body of a grown woman already, and best of all were those sad, blue eyes that let you know how much she cared about you, even when she didn't say a word.

Actually, she talked a lot, considering that she was deaf. Her voice was a little strange, kind of flat and nasal, but, to me, it was the most wonderful sound I'd ever heard.

"Lonek," she said, calling me by the Polish name I was using. "I'm sorry things aren't going well. You suffer so much, Lonek." When she spoke, her eyes filled with tears. One rolled along her pink cheek and disappeared somewhere down her ruffly blouse.

Andzia's mother wore an apron with big pockets. All day long, she dropped food into those pockets, without anybody noticing. Then, at the end of the day, Andzia brought the food to me. Because she was deaf, she explained, she came only at night. The idea was, what if someone called for her during the day, and she couldn't hear it? The person would find out our secret for sure. Our secret. I liked that.

I wanted to tell her that I would hear if someone called. But her company was every bit as important to me as the food and water she brought, and I didn't want her to be nervous while she was here. Anyway, during the day, I could read. At night, I couldn't do anything. So, when Andzia came with her little lantern and covered plate of food, it was like Chanukah and Purim rolled into one, every night.

# Fay

When the harvest was over, Mr. Dudek let me come downstairs every once in a while. The idea was to make me more comfortable, but I was eager to help around the house and earn my keep any way I could. Each day, I hoped I would be called down. Joining the family became like a drug for me. I knew how dangerous it was, but I could never refuse it.

No one, I learned, had seen my brother shot. That did not mean that he was alive, but it made me think that someday I might be sitting with him again, just like with the Dudeks, in our own household. It was a crumb of hope that nourished my fragile belief in the future.

One evening after supper, I was sitting with the family, mending some old clothing. I was suffering from a bad cough, and Mrs. Dudek was in the middle of explaining an old Polish remedy, something about wrapping the throat overnight in a wet rag. Suddenly, we heard a loud pounding on the door. I held my breath and looked at her. She looked at her husband. He cocked his head toward the closet, and I tiptoed across the room and closed it behind me without a sound.

The closet was musty and cold. I heard the door open and the clomping of official boots on the dirt floor. Then I heard men speaking Polish, so I knew it wasn't the Nazi SS. At least we could be thankful for that.

After a minute or two, the dust of the closet settled in my throat and lungs. I needed to cough. If I did not do it soon, I would surely choke. I cursed myself for not having taken my cup of hot tea with me. It was still sitting on the rough-hewn table by the fire.

Dudek poured the men whiskey and casually asked what brought them out at such a late hour.

"We had news that some Jewish families were hiding in the village," one of them said. "We're on our way to check them out. Since we were in the neighborhood, we thought we'd stop by."

"Yeah," the other one added. "We figured they'd let down their guard at night, thinking that no one would be checking for them."

I did not hear Mr. Dudek's reply. My entire being was focused on clearing my throat. Then everybody started laughing, and Dudek cried out, "To our health!" It was just the noise I needed to release a quick cough.

I have no idea how long they were there. But when they left, I was exhausted, and my face was a deep crimson. I resolved to be more careful in the future.

Months went by, and I was out of money. The Dudeks decided that I was more trouble than I was worth and that I would have to go. They had been more than kind to me. But, somehow, I had hoped that I could stay with them a while longer.

Valerja Dudek's sister Kazia lived in the same village. She took me in for a few weeks. But Kazia was young and careless, and before long people started to talk about me. I knew I should move on, but it was winter, and I couldn't bear to be without a roof over my head. So, when Kazia told me that she would keep me longer if I could pay her, I devised a plan.

I told her to go to the Kwasniaks at our house back in town. Maybe they would at least send over some clothing or bedding. Much as I did not trust Mr. Kwasniak, I had no choice.

To my disappointment, Kazia came back empty-handed. But then she said that Rózia Kwasniak was going to come on her own. Of course, Rózia's husband had warned Kazia against keeping Jews. But, thank goodness, neither of the women paid any attention to him.

I could hardly wait until Rózia's visit the next day. When we fell into each other's arms at last, I almost felt, for a few minutes, that I was safe.

She held my face in her hands and kissed both my cheeks. "I am so happy that you are alive!" she said, holding me close. "Here are a few things to tide you over. Just tell me what else you need, and I will bring it to you."

Rózia told me about my family's death, what she had heard from the policeman who was present at their execution. We wept together, the tears spilling down our cheeks. I asked about my brother, but she said she had no idea what had happened to him. Then she told me about other people. Our neighbors, the most prominent family in town, had committed suicide. They were lucky to have been able to buy poison. It was an expensive commodity, much in demand.

154

When Rózia left, she promised to return soon. Much as I appreciated what she had done for me, I could not tell her that I doubted I would still be there much longer.

Winter had arrived with full force, and snow blanketed the countryside. The house was warm, however, and each night I prayed that I would be able to stay just a day or two longer.

Then Kazia informed me that the Gestapo had pulled a Jewish family from a peasant's cellar and shot them all. The story was her way of telling me to move on. Unfortunately, anyone in his right mind was likely to feel the same way.

# Leo

It was maybe a week or two after I got to Mr. Chmura. He sat watching me while I did my stretches and ran around the barn. I knew he had something on his mind, but I couldn't figure out what. If he was having such a hard time telling me, I decided, bending at my waist and dropping my hands to the floor, it must be something pretty bad. I was sure he wasn't able to keep me anymore. What else could be so hard to talk about?

After I ate, he told me he had something to say. Here it comes, I thought, my stomach churning. We leaned back against the dry straw, and I took a piece to use to pick my teeth.

"My child," he said, putting his hand on my shoulder. In the dimness of the lantern light, I hadn't noticed until then that he was crying. The last man I had seen cry was my father, and the sight turned my insides to dust.

I tried to make it easy for him. "I have to go, right? Is that what you want to tell me?"

His sad eyes widened. "No, not at all," he said. "You are welcome to stay here as long as you need to."

"What is it, then?"

But the minute the words left my mouth, I knew. I knew as surely as if it had been written on the walls of the barn. I said, "My family."

He nodded. I waited for him to say something else, but he didn't.

"What happened?" I asked at last. "Please, tell me everything."

He shuddered. When he spoke, his eyes were glued on the cow, as if that stupid animal were as interested in the death of my family as I was.

Then he said, "They rounded up all the Jews in Kanczuga into the main square. Those who didn't come, they shot in their homes. The rest they took to the old synagogue."

156

"The old synagogue," I said. "That wouldn't hold everybody."

"They weren't exactly sitting like lords and ladies," he said, a little harshly. In a softer voice, he added, "Then they took out the men and—shot them."

"Shot them? Where? Right there outside the synagogue?"

Bless Mr. Chmura. He knew why I had to know every detail. He said, "No, my son. They took them to the Jewish cemetery."

"And the women?"

"Shot the next day.

"And—they buried them there?"

"They shot them by a pit."

In my mind I saw the same pit I'd imagined when the survivor came to Kanczuga and told us about the massacre in his town. I heard the screams and the shots. So real they were to me that I almost looked around to see what the commotion was about.

"It's not possible," I said. "It's not possible that they're no longer alive. Just like that. It can't be."

He swallowed once. Twice. Then he said, "If only I could have—" His voice trailed off. We both knew there was nothing for him to say. After a few minutes, he asked, "Do you want me to go now?"

I knew he would have been happy to have me cry into his arms. He was an emotional person, and, except for his masculine looks, he reminded me more of my mother than of my father. But, somehow, hugging him seemed like an insult to my dead parents.

"Sure," I said. "I'm okay."

Still he couldn't meet my eyes. To the cow he said, "I don't mind staying with you a little longer, if you need me to."

"I'm fine, really," I said. "Good night, Mr. Chmura."

"Good night, son."

I climbed back to my hiding place under the eaves and stared up at my darkened pinhole for a long time. I knew I should be crying, or praying at least. But I felt nothing. My heart was as dry as the straw I lay on, and as dumb as the cow down below.

# Fay

I was enshrouded in snow the instant I stepped out in it. In vain, I searched for footprints, but the driving wind covered any prints as soon as they were made. Five minutes could not have passed before I was completely lost. For all I knew, I was traveling in one big circle and would end up at the end of the day back at the door of the woman who had thrown me out.

My teeth started to chatter, and I shivered violently. Before I left, Kazia had sold me a warm woolen stole, but I had only a thin kerchief on my head and my ridiculous high heels. I fought back the tears welling up in my eyes. All I needed, I thought wryly, was for them to freeze on my cheeks.

I was lucky to have spent six months in so few houses, I knew. But my luck could not hold forever. Now, I had to think where else I could go. And how I could get there in all this snow.

I remembered that, of all our friends in the surrounding villages, one shoemaker had been especially kind. I made up my mind to get to his house no matter what. That house became a beacon for me, a place in which I instilled all my hopes.

Rewer was a good person, and so was his wife, Marysia, with whom he was very much in love. The year before, they had returned from France, where he had made a little money. Rewer had bought a piece of land. Last I heard, he was building a stable for their cow, which had always lived with them inside the house.

As I walked, the snowfall grew lighter, until, by the time I reached Rewer's village, it had subsided altogether. Sometime in the early evening, I knocked on the door of the hut.

"Rewer, it's Faiga Rosenbluth!" I whispered, when he asked who was there. "Remember the daughter of the owner of the Jewish store where you bought your leather?"

He opened the door at once and stood perfectly still, taking in the picture of my misery. Torn stockings, soggy shoes, wet clothing sticking to my sides. Marysia joined him. They both gaped at me in silence. It was as if no one wanted to be the first to speak.

Finally, Rewer motioned me inside. He turned to his wife. "Marysia, you know those boots I made for you that you don't wear anymore? Bring them here, love."

When Marysia left, Rewer said, "You know we can't keep you very long. We already have too many people living in this house. But the least we can do is help you get a little warmer. Then we'll find you someplace more permanent."

After Marysia returned with the boots, Rewer took me to the stable. I slept there quite contentedly, nestled in the warm straw.

The next day, I helped around the house and in the stable. After having lived among peasants for six months, I knew my way around a farm.

Meanwhile, Rewer tried to find me a place to stay. It wasn't easy. I had no money, so people had little incentive to risk their lives.

I lay awake night after night, racking my brain for villagers who might be willing to help. Then I recalled that my parents had given our sewing machine to Zajac. Despite the fact that he hadn't taken in my parents, he had been a good customer and an honest man, and my father had trusted him.

I told Rewer, and he had one of his farmhands take me over there in a sled. If the man agreed to return the sewing machine, Rewer said, the farmhand's parents would keep me for six months.

Six months, I thought. That would make it summertime before I would be on my own. And summer would be a lot easier. If need be, I could always sleep in the fields.

We set off on the sled late one afternoon. The trip was short, but the snow made the roads almost impassable. By the time we reached the house, my heart was pounding, and the poor horse was snorting furiously.

I rapped on the door with a steady hand. I was dressed like a farm-girl at last, and my feet were nice and toasty in my hand-me-down boots.

But the minute I saw the man's face, I lost my confidence. He looked down at me with an expression of disdain.

"We have nothing of yours," he said, when I explained to him what I'd come for.

I could see immediately that there was no reason to argue. As I turned to go, he said, "You know I could report you to the police. But I am a good person and will not do it. Just don't ever come here again."

When the door banged shut, I was so shaken that I didn't notice the three teenaged boys walking toward me until I was almost on top of them. One of them was a customer from the store. When I said hello to him, he grimaced and turned away.

Then the biggest of the boys said in a menacing voice, "We know who you are. You'd better come with us."

At first I was afraid and wondered whether my sled driver would protect me if I called for help. But then a strange aura of calm settled over me. What, I thought, was the worst that could happen to me? I'd already lost everything I cared about.

So I took a step toward the boy and said, "Do you really want to have me on your conscience? Will that make you happy? I will die, but you will have to go on living right here, in this town. You will marry and raise children here. And, for the rest of your life, every time you pass this house, you will think of me."

I paused just for a moment. In the darkness, I couldn't gauge his reaction. "I have nothing to lose," I continued. "My family is dead. And, sooner or later, I will meet the same fate. But I wouldn't want to die by your hands. I am no stranger to you."

Then I sighed for dramatic effect, and said, "It is your choice. Take me to the police if you must. Only I ask you—"

They did not wait for me to finish. With bowed heads, they skulked away behind the house.

Only after I reached the sled and told the driver to leave did I realize that my legs were shaking. But I had no time to contemplate my success. I had to find somewhere to stay before I froze to death.

Door after door was shut in my face, until I grew so cold and depressed I thought of simply lying down in the snow and giving up. But then I found myself at the Skoczylases. I had known them most of my life and had every reason to believe that they would help. They did not disappoint me. Mrs. Skoczylas took me into her arms, and I cried into her broad bosom. When I had told her everything through my sobs, she fed me a hot meal. Then she took my clothing to wash and gave me warm water for a bath.

My hiding place was in the stable, where I lay in the straw and covered myself with my stole to keep warm. We agreed that, if I were discovered, I would say that I had walked in without asking anyone.

That first night, the cat curled up next to me. Even the dogs in that household were friendly. They knew me so well that they did not bark when they sensed me coming.

I thanked Mrs. Skoczylas a thousand times before she left me for her own bed. Then I breathed a prayer of gratitude, tickled the cat behind the ears one last time, and settled into a deep, dreamless sleep.

The Skoczylases were as smart as they were kind. They were known throughout the village as excellent businesspeople, and they put me to work the very next morning. I was grateful. We quickly determined that the best way for me to support myself was to knit sweaters for the two adults and two boys. All those years working by my mother's side were now keeping me alive, and I silently thanked her every day. Because I had no light apart from the sun, I worked from daybreak to sunset.

My imagination soared in that cheery little barn. I knitted sweater after sweater in the most beautiful designs. But when I had made one for every member of the family, I was told that I would have to go.

The next night, Mr. Skoczylas called me into the house, as he had often done. This time, two shoemakers were sitting in the room. I knew them well from the store and greeted them warmly.

Mr. Skoczylas sat in his usual chair by the fire and shook his head. "What shall we do with you?" he asked me. "You have been here almost a month, and still the war is not over."

Then he turned to the shoemakers. "We can't let her wander out in the cold, my friends. Juziu, what about if you take her in for a while? Then Bolek, you can keep her after that. This damned war has got to end sometime."

That same night, I hugged each of the Skoczylases and went home with my new host. I knew very well that he would not have taken me if Mr. Skoczylas had not talked him into it. I would be grateful to that couple forever.

Mr. Juziu had three little daughters, and we all slept together in the attic, on warm beds of hay. Once more, my early training came in handy. I taught my new friends how to sew and knit, unraveling many sweaters and making them over until they looked like new.

Then, one day, Juziu announced that he was sending me over to Bolek. I stayed with him for a few weeks, until he too told me it was time to move on.

"It's nothing personal," he stammered, hanging his head until I could see the shiny bald spot beneath the sparse gray hair. "But I just can't keep

161

you forever. It's too much responsibility. Too much worry for my children. You understand?"

I told him not to blame himself. Winter was rolling up its white carpet, in preparation for the dance of spring. I was well fed and well rested. Most important, I knew that, in case of emergency, I could always go back to one of these three families. And that knowledge was the greatest gift of all.

# Leo

They were grilling kielbasa outside, and that smell was like heaven! My mouth watered so much that if Mr. Chmura hadn't brought me some, I might've risked everything and ransacked the house for it.

So Mr. Chmura hands me this plate with two sausages on it, these two fat brown fingers. And, of course, he doesn't think twice about it, has no idea what a big deal this stupid piece of meat is for me. Mr. Chmura is a religious man, but he's religious Catholic, and they can eat anything, except meat on Fridays and whatever it is they give up at Lent. But we Jews are obsessed with which animals are kosher and which are not, what is *milchik*, or milk, what is *fleishik*, or meat, and that kind of thing.

Mr. C. is chatting away about the war and the weather, and, for all I've been starving for the sound of a human voice, I can't concentrate on a word he's saying. I just keep thinking, Treyf, treyf, this is as treyf as you can get. What would Mamche say?

I know exactly what Mamche would say. But Mamche also said to stay alive, no matter what. So I pick up one of the fat brown rolls in my pale skinny fingers, and I bite into it, and the blood snakes down my chin. I've stared at the thing so long that it's no longer warm, but it's so delicious, I hardly notice. I was ordered to stay alive. So I eat the kielbasa for my mother, and my father, and my grandparents, and my sisters. I dedicate this blood sausage to the Jewish people.

# Fay

Left, right, left, right, forcing one dusty boot ahead of the other. All that spring and summer, I walked after dark to avoid suspicion, staying clear of the road whenever I could. When I found an empty barn, I would duck in unnoticed long past dark and leave first thing in the morning. I bathed in the lakes and ate from the fields, or wherever someone was kind enough to give me food.

It was a beautiful night in Indian summer, which the Poles call *babie lato*. I was weary and damp with sweat, but not uncomfortable. The moon was a half smile perched in a star-strung sky. I craned my neck as I made my way among the potatoes, thinking how the stars must look the same above my parents' house in Kanczuga, not five miles away.

I came upon an abandoned hut perched along a lovely, tree-lined lake. Sitting cross-legged on the dirt floor, I dined on gritty carrots, sunflower seeds, and rye. They were not as good as the peas, carrots, and corn I'd had the night before, but they filled my empty stomach. I ate the rye right out of the husk, just like the seeds. It was chewy and tasteless, but I felt lucky to have it.

After resting a while, I went back outside, peeled off my ragged clothes, and took a swim. The water was warm, and I splashed merrily in my luxurious bath. Although I kept an ear out for trouble, I felt relaxed and safe. In the country, everyone goes to bed early. The night belonged to me.

Then I heard the voices. They were quite clear, and not very far away. My mouth went dry with fear. If I left the lake, they would hear me. I had only one choice: to hold my breath and hide underwater.

Careful not to splash now, I took a deep breath and slowly sank beneath the surface. I stayed there as long as I could, with only one thought: my clothing left on the bank.

When I came up for air, I had no idea what to expect. I spun around in a wary circle, expecting the worst. But, to my immense relief, they were gone.

I was so frightened that, tired as I was, I was afraid to return to the hut. Instead I bedded down in a beet field, my woolen stole propped beneath my head for a pillow. On every side were dense plants, swathed in the early morning mist.

I hunkered in between the rows of green, alert to the smallest sound of life. How quickly I had become used to danger! For nineteen years, all I had known of death was the passing of my beloved grandparents, and the worst threat I had faced was my parents' disapproval when I went out dancing. Now, in the space of a few years, my thoughts had become filled with police and executions. I hardly recognized myself anymore. I could not shut my eyes. Instead, I sang myself to sleep with some of the songs of my childhood.

> Lomir zikh iberbetn, iberbetn,
> Shtel dem samovar;
> Lomir zikh iberbetn,
> Zay zhe nit keyn nar,
>
> Lomir zikh iberbetn, iberbetn
> Koyf mir a por marantsn;
> Lomir zikh iberbetn,
> Lomir geyn tantsn.
>
> Lomir zikh iberbetn, iberbetn,
> Vos shteystu bay der tir?
> Lomir zikh iberbetn,
> Kib a kuk oyf mir.
>
> [Let's make up!
> Heat up the samovar.
> Let's make up
> And don't be foolish!
>
> Let's make up!
> Buy me oranges.
> Let's make up
> And go dancing.

Let's make up!
Why are you standing at the door?
Let's make up
And look at me.]

By the time I drifted off, it was nearly dawn, time for night creatures like me to hide from the sun.

The next day, I approached a house in the village of Sietesz, just before dark. I had walked through heavy rain for hours and didn't have the strength to take another step. I do not know what came over me. I just walked right up to the door and pulled it open.

As soon as I was inside, a woman approached me. She was round and pale, with a stern, tired face. She reminded me of one of my aunts.

"What do you want?" she asked.

And, just like that, I burst into tears. I was as shocked as she. Since leaving the Skoczylases, I had not cried once, and now the tears were pouring forth in a torrent.

The woman reached for my hand and led me into the other room. She closed the door behind her and said, "Cry all you want. I will bring you some food."

I stayed with the Swietliks for quite some time and became very close to them. Unfortunately, their house was so near the road that their neighbors would become suspicious at the smallest thing. So we could not let down our guard for an instant.

Soon it was harvest time again, and the family left early in the morning and returned late in the afternoon. The houses were not locked, and people could stop in without warning. When I learned that my hosts also owned the isolated hut I'd slept in by the lake, I told them we would probably all be safer if I stayed there.

All went well until the harvest was in. Then, the fields were as naked as I had been in that luminous lake. I could no longer stay in them, and passersby were sure to use the hut as shelter from the cold or rain. Neither could I go back to the Skoczylases and their neighbors. Those places I was saving for the winter.

Instead, I headed for the woods. I slept on soft beds of pine needles and watched in fascination as the many species of birds and other creatures of the forest raised their families. Once I touched a nest, to see how it was made. The birds scurried out and built another one in a different place. I understood. The parents were just looking after their babies, trying to keep them safe.

One evening, I found a watchman's hut made from branches and lined with dry leaves. I was tempted to hide there for a while, but it was too obvious a shelter. I decided to use it only in case of rain.

But it rained that very night, and I made myself comfortable in my romantic hideaway. I had eaten a good supper at a farmer's house earlier in the day, and he had given me a piece of bread for the road. So I was well fed and warm. I drifted off to sleep, but, as usual, it was a light slumber, watchful and wary.

And, then, as if in a dream, I heard Yiddish. Could it possibly be? I had not heard my language for a year. Was I talking to myself, or were there others like me, also hiding in the countryside?

The rain had stopped, and the air smelled fresh and newly bathed. Slowly, I tiptoed into the clearing. There, sitting on the ground, were two young boys. When I introduced myself, they said they had been told to look out for me.

I asked them whether they knew anything about Luzer. I did not know why, except that the sight of these two young boys made me miss him more than I could bear.

They shook their heads. I was the only Jew they had heard of for a long time. Everyone else, as far as they knew, was gone.

I had not realized how hopeful I had been until they said that. Then I felt an emptiness so powerful I excused myself for a minute to calm down.

When I returned to them, we talked for hours about our hardships. They kept asking me, "Is there any hope for us? Will the war ever end?"

I shrugged. "Maybe we will be the lucky ones," I said. "Maybe someday, we will enjoy our freedom again. All we can do is try. If we give up now, we are only helping our enemies."

When morning came, we hugged and went our separate ways. After a few steps, I stopped and turned to watch my two new friends disappear into the forest. Speaking my language again reminded me of who I really was, of what my life had once been. When they left, it was as if they were taking a piece of me with them. I wondered whether I would ever get it back.

# Leo

I was still sleeping when Mr. Chmura pulled up the boards of my hiding place. In the lantern light, his eyes looked very tired.

"What's the matter?" I asked. I had grown so used to our routine that any change made me expect the worst.

"I was about to ask you the same thing," he said, dropping down onto a block of hay. "You were screaming."

"Screaming? But it couldn't have been me! I was sound asleep!"

He nodded, his face grim. "I'm afraid that's the problem," he said. "You must have had a nightmare. You were obviously screaming in your sleep."

I shook my head. "I've never done that before!"

"Maybe you have," he said. "I've heard strange noises before, late at night, but I never thought it was you. Tonight, though, there was no mistaking it. What I heard was the cry of a man in trouble."

If I hadn't been so worried, I would have grinned at the word "man." I might have the troubles of a man, but no one had ever called me one, at least not to my face.

"Did anybody else hear me?"

"I don't know. My wife is asleep, but I didn't check on all of the children. Maybe, come morning, they'll think that they were having a bad dream, too."

"What can I do?" I asked. "Sleep with a rag in my teeth?"

He shook his head. "I don't think that'll help. Do you know what it is you dreamed? Why you screamed, I mean?"

I shrugged. I knew; of course I knew, but I couldn't tell him. I knew the bloody faces I had seen, the outstretched hands. I remembered the screams I'd heard. How could I have known they were mine?

"I don't know what to say," he continued. "If I were you, having seen what you'd seen at your age, I'd probably be screaming while I was wide awake. I don't know how to tell you to stop screaming in your sleep. But if you don't, we're going to be in serious trouble, you and I."

I nodded. "Of course," I said. "I understand. I'll do my best."

He reached over and hugged me. In his big arms, I felt like a scarecrow. Or like the orphan I was.

"My poor boy," he said, his voice breaking. "No one should have to endure such torment. I hope to God that someday soon it will all end, and you will have a normal, healthy life."

"Thank you, Mr. Chmura," I said. "I hope so, too."

When he was gone, I tried to get back to sleep. Then my eyes flew open as it hit me: How could I ever sleep again? What if I started screaming? And what if I fell asleep during the day and screamed? What if someone was right outside the door when it happened? How could Mr. Chmura possibly keep up our secret if I went screaming my head off in the middle of the day?

Now I was more scared than ever. It was one thing to be worried about what might happen to you when you were awake. Things you could control, or things you could at least think how to react to. But when you're afraid of what might happen during sleep, you're lost. Because that's something you can't do a thing about.

And here I thought I'd already lost everything.

So, even though I knew it was useless, I tried to stay awake. I told myself every story I'd ever heard, sang every song under my breath. I cracked my knuckles about a thousand times. I even tried to exercise laying in my little cubbyhole, but there wasn't much chance of that.

Then I had the bright idea of starting to count. I guess I didn't realize that that's a great way to send yourself off to dreamland. Because I was out cold before I reached a hundred.

At least, when I asked Mr. C. the next night, he said he hadn't heard a sound.

# Fay

As bad as things got, the worst was moving from one village to the next. If I stayed in one place, I could always duck behind a house or slip into a barn if I needed to. But when I was in between, all roads looked the same. I would ask directions before setting out, but I could not seem to keep all those lefts and rights and curves and lakes in my head. And, of course, I could not ask anybody. For one thing, I was afraid that someone would recognize me and turn me in. For another, I traveled at night, when very few people were out.

When I lost my way, I would stop walking and lie in a field until the next evening, when I would try again. How can I explain the feeling of hiding in the dirt for twelve hours, waiting for nightfall to straighten out your legs and find something to eat? I was just another living thing, part of the earth. Except that everything around me was growing and thriving, while I felt as if the life were being strangled out of me, drop by drop.

Winter came once more, and with it those impenetrable snows, as high as my chest. One snowstorm fell on top of the last, with no one clearing the roads in between. I made my way as best I could, trying to concentrate on the beauty of the snowflakes, the cold breath that sprayed from my mouth in a frosty film, the icicles that clung to the stripped tree branches like folds of a satin shawl draped across bare arms.

Everything was white, every rooftop, every tree, every place my foot fell. With my warm boots and stole, I was not cold, but the effort of pushing through the drifts was doubly exhausting. One night I just sat down in the snow, unable to move another step. I tried to stay awake, fearful that I would freeze to death overnight. But I could not help myself. My lids closed as surely as if a curtain had been drawn across my eyes.

When I awoke, the sun was overhead, and I was surrounded by frozen white walls. The heat of my body had apparently melted the snow around me, encasing me in a little igloo. It was just the right size for me to sleep in a sitting position.

Comfortable as I was, I shook with fear when I stood up. I had been lucky, not brave, not clever, just lucky to be alive. The next time I fell asleep in the snow, who knew what would happen to me?

Late that night, I was on the road back to Dudek's farm. I had no other choice. It was already quite late, and I had been turned away at door after door, when I heard rough singing behind me. My first thought was to run. But that would only attract suspicion.

I decided to turn at the first crossroad. But I never got the chance.

"Where are you going so late?" the drunken voice asked me.

"It's none of your business," I replied. "Just as it is none of my business where you are off to."

My knees were shaking so much, I don't know how I managed to keep upright.

Now the man was beside me. His nose was red, and his eyes were unnaturally bright. He looked as if he hadn't shaved in a week. I could smell the bitter odor of whiskey on his breath.

His eyes narrowed now, and he reached his right hand into his back pocket.

Oh, dear God, I thought. He has a gun. More than a year on the road, and here I am, in as much danger as when I started. I lived another year to die like a dog on the street.

"Little miss," the man growled, "if you don't tell me who are and what you're doing here, I am going to shoot you, sure as I am standing here."

I put my hands on my hips and stood in the middle of the road as if I owned it.

"Do I have a choice?" I asked. "Whether I tell you or not, don't you already know? What young woman would walk alone at this late hour? I know who I am, and so do you. But where I am going, I can't tell you, because I don't know myself. Maybe it's just as well that you will put an end to my suffering. This is as good a place to die as any, and I am so tired, I can't go on anymore. Let me die under the stars, under God's shimmering sky."

The man took a step closer, pulled out a flashlight from his jacket, and directed it on my face. He turned pale, and his jaw dropped. It was as if he were sobering up before my eyes.

"Miss Rosenbluth?" he whispered. "Can you ever forgive me? If I had known who you were, I would never have said those things."

I said something noncommital, and he turned to go on his way. But, before too long, he was beside me again, panting in the cold night air. Again he asked my forgiveness. Again I said, "Sure, sure, don't worry. It's all right."

I hadn't gone ten paces when he was back once more, apologizing. In all, he came back three times before he was satisfied that I would forgive him. He told me that he was the mayor of that village, and he assured me that only good people lived there. At last, he wished me luck and disappeared into the night.

Maciej Dudek came to the door when I knocked, took one long look at me, and barred me from entering the house.

"Oh, you're still alive?" he asked. "Good for you. But, if you've got nothing for us, we've got nothing for you."

From there, I wandered to the poorest house in the village. It was barely a house at all, just a few walls slapped together from yellow soil and straw, with a roof of branches and leaves. But they gave me some bread and fat and brought some straw up to the attic for me to sleep on. In one room, they slept on beds of straw themselves, with no sheets. In the other, their cow placidly chewed her cud.

They had nothing, this couple. They could not go to church because their clothing was too ragged. Their two boys went to school only in summer, because they had no shoes. When I arrived, their cow was pregnant, so they had no milk and existed on potatoes and cabbage. Five of their children had died before their first birthdays.

And yet that home was the happiest I had seen in all my travels. Every morning I heard the husband, Andrzej, whistling as he readied himself for the day. They were Polish nationals, proud to live in their own little house. No power could chase them away, they said defiantly. No Hitler was big enough to throw them off their land.

I set about making sweaters for their boys out of the same twine we had used for wrapping packages at home. Andrezj hated Jews. But, as a Christian, he said, he felt sorry for me and wanted to help. So I could stay with them for a while.

In my travels, it was the only visit I was ever to cut short voluntarily. My bed was a so full of bugs and lice that I could not sleep. By the time I finished the sweaters, every inch of me was red and sore from scratching.

I left to go back to the Skoczylases, where I stayed just long enough to wash and boil my clothes and heal my sorry skin.

# Leo

I was laying flat on my back, like always. Making out the newspaper one word at a time through the pinhole of light. The Germans had had some losses, and I was feeling pretty good.

Suddenly I felt something scurry past my leg. I was so surprised that I jumped about a mile, or at least I would have, if I hadn't had a roof eighteen inches above my head.

I lay still, waiting for whatever it was to come back. And, in a couple of minutes, there it was, sniffing and crawling around my newspaper. Through the string of light I could just make it out: a tiny black field mouse.

A mouse! You couldn't have made me happier if you'd given me a dog. In fact, how could you keep a dog in that box I lived in? But a mouse was just perfect.

I'd saved a few bites of bread from Andzia's dinner the night before. Slowly, since I didn't want to scare him away, I slipped my hand into my pocket. But the little guy was way ahead of me. He was already nosing around in there for a treat. I held the bread up to him, and he put out his little arms. Then I led him back to the thimbleful of light on my newspaper. When he was completely involved with the bread, I took hold of his little body. He kicked his feet in panic, and I was torn with emotions. How could I, the most powerless person on earth, play god to a little mouse? It felt good and disgusting at the same time. It even crossed my mind, just for a second, how it would feel to crush the helpless thing.

But I was only moving the paper. Quick as I could, I resettled the little fellow on my chest.

"Feel my heart?" I whispered. "Now, you know I'm a good person. I would never, never hurt you, little fella."

While he devoured the bread, I stroked him with one finger. At first, he seemed nervous, but then he began to settle down.

"Some day we'll get out of here," I said. "You and me. And I'll have my own store. And I'll have four or five kids. And a wife, of course. And a nice house, with two stories, just like the mayor. Jews or no Jews, you and me, we're going to survive. And no one is ever going to treat us like mice again! No, sir, we're going to stand up to 'em. We'll show 'em!"

The mouse looked up at me, startled. So excited was I that I'd probably pressed down on him a little too hard. He dropped the last few flakes of bread and scampered into a corner, just out of reach. How could I blame him? We mice had to look out for ourselves.

# Fay

Winter melted into spring, which softened into summer, and I was still on the road, sometimes chased by angry dogs, sometimes fed by gracious peasants. I never pleaded or cried to be let in. I was too disgusted. I had had enough.

Somebody told me that one of the villages was owned by a princess. She lived in a castle, supposedly, and was very good to the poor. I decided to see whether she would hire me.

I had to go in the daytime, of course, but I figured it was worth the risk. So I washed myself as best I could, combed back my hair into one long pigtail, and set out for the village.

The castle was beautiful, like something out of a fairy tale, with high turrets and huge iron doors. My heart pounding, I entered the anteroom, where a man in a fancy suit asked me to sit down. I tried to sit like a lady, but my nervousness made me fidget.

At last, a proper-looking young woman came out to ask my name and what I wanted. She was also dressed in a suit and spoke quickly, as if she barely had the time to wait for my response.

"Please, ma'am," I said. "I would like to see the princess herself, if it is at all possible."

"The princess doesn't see people before ten o'clock," she replied with a frown. She consulted the big clock in the corner and added, "It's only eight-thirty now. You can come back or take a seat in the waiting room."

I decided to wait. What else did I have to do? As I sat, the room filled with people. It seemed to me that everyone knew me. Some people even called out my name, but no one came over to have a conversation. They just wanted to look at a once-fashionable, coddled Jew, now down on her luck.

Sometime after ten, the lady in the suit ushered me into another room

175

and closed the door behind her. I gasped. The walls were trimmed in brocade. The furniture was more luxurious than anything I had ever seen.

While I was taking it all in, another door opened, and in walked a goddess, wearing a simple, sophisticated dress and leading two big dogs. She lowered herself into a delicate chair, and the dogs lay down beside her, one on each side, like loyal sentinels. Her sweet perfume filled the room with the delicate aroma of wildflowers.

I stood up when she entered, but she smiled and waved for me to sit.

"So tell me, my child, what I can do for you."

"I am looking for work," I said. "I don't expect charity."

She smiled, sadly this time, and shook her head. "I have enough workers," she said. "But I advise you not to go out in the open. Everyone knows you here. And you look and talk every bit a Jew. God willing, this war will be over soon. In the meantime, hide yourself during the day."

She led me into the kitchen and gave me a cake and two big oranges. Then she told the cook to feed me lunch and disappeared behind a side door. When she returned, she handed me a small bundle of clothing and wished me luck.

I should not have been surprised. This woman owed me nothing. But, for days afterward, I could not shake my disappointment.

One night I got terribly lost. I was dizzy from wandering around in ever smaller circles, searching for a particular house. Angry and tired, I slipped into a barn to rest.

As soon as I entered, the barn grew lighter, and I felt a presence behind me. I wheeled around to find two men holding a lantern.

"Who is it, and what are you doing here?" they asked.

I approached them with my hands outstretched. "I am not a thief. I just want to rest a little. If you want me to go, I will leave."

"Oh!" laughed the taller one, who was holding the lantern. "It's you! You will never get out of here alive, you dirty Jew. Your father took everything we had because we couldn't afford to pay him for his stinking Jew leather. We'll fix you! We're calling the police!"

With that, they closed the barn door behind them. The only sound on earth was the ringing in my ears, my constant companion. I dropped my bundle onto the dirt floor and flopped down beside it. Then I pulled out my mother's picture and held it in my hands. The barn was too dark even to make out the outline of her features, but I figured that if I were to die, I wanted to have her close to me.

I was resigned to my death. Over the past year I had suffered so much, and for what? I was so terribly tired; I was just glad it was over. No more wondering where to go. No more constant vigilance. No more farmers who told me that they hated Jews but that, as good Christians, they were honor-bound to help me. Soon I could close my eyes forever and be at peace.

Dear God, I prayed, Whatever happens to me, please keep my brother safe. And if the police come to take me away, let them finish me off here. Please don't let them parade me around my hometown first.

As soon as I said the words, I knew that I would run, and they would have to shoot me before I ever got near Kanczuga.

The barn was warm, and I had been walking all day. Without even re-alizing that my eyes were closing, I nodded off to sleep.

# Leo

When Mr. Chmura came for me one hot summer night, I was even more antsy than usual. I stretched from side to side, then ran in place, feeling my tight muscles begin to loosen, my shallow breath start to grow deep and full.

"I can't take it anymore, Mr. Chmura," I said. "I've got to go out and try to make it on my own."

"You mustn't do that, son. Remember, you made a promise to your mother to stay safe."

"But it's no use! Hitler's going to win the war. I know it. I read the papers, remember?"

"Now, now, my son, the papers don't know everything. Didn't you hear the Russians shooting at the Germans today?"

"Mr. Chmura, excuse me, but I'm not an idiot. That was your kids playing with firecrackers."

"No, it was the Russians! You wait; soon you'll leave here a free man, go back out into the world with your head held high. Now won't that be worth all this trouble?"

I shook my head. "Nothing is worth this. You can't know! You don't spend your life in here! You can't possibly know what it's like!"

I knew I was being rude, that I had no right to speak to him that way. But it was like a dam bursting. I couldn't take the words back, and I couldn't stop the flow of misery pouring out of my mouth.

"I feel like a cow in here," I continued. "Like a vegetable, in storage for the summer. Like a piece of farm machinery. What kind of life is that? How can anyone be expected to live like this?"

He rubbed his chin. "Well," he sighed, "at least it is life. Plenty of Jews don't even have that anymore."

"THIS — IS — NOT — LIFE!"

178

I had never spoken so loudly in there, and I know he wasn't happy about it. But, good man that he was, he didn't say a word. He just drew me to him and gave me a hug. What else could he do? And there in that barn, in the middle of the night, in the middle of the war, I sobbed into the arms of the only man on earth who cared whether I lived or died. That night, I cried down to my bones.

# Fay

I opened my eyes, my heart in my throat even before I remembered where I was. A sliver of sunlight filled the space between the barn door and the dirt below. I approached the door and gave it a gentle push. To my amazement, it sprang open. I walked out into the sunshine, looking to either side, fully expecting to find someone waiting for me with a shotgun. But I was alone, free to move on and find another place to sleep, another problem to worry about.

I had not put one foot in front of the other before I began to cry. Whether it was from loneliness, from disappointment at not having it all finally over, or a delayed reaction to the previous night's terror hardly mattered. The pain was so great that I was afraid I would attract more attention than usual with my keening. I hated to impose on their goodness, but when I felt this bad, the only thing that helped was a visit to the Skoczylases.

As soon as I crossed the familiar threshold, I felt lighter. Mother Skoczylas milked the cows, and I sat beside her, sobbing into the straw at our feet. Then she took me inside and gave me food, hot water for a bath, and a place to stay for the night. Most important of all, the family gave me the courage to stay alive. I was careful not to stay too long. I wanted to be sure I always had a place to return to.

The following weeks were cold and wet. But even if the weather had been beautiful, I would not have been safe in the open. The Gestapo was scouring the villages for the last remaining Jews. Anyone who helped them could be shot on the spot. I slept in barns or attics whenever I could, making a hole in the hay to cover myself.

One night, I settled into a bed of straw in the attic of the Swietliks, farmers who had put me up earlier in my travels. I blessed their family and thanked God for guiding me to them. I was just drifting off to sleep when I heard voices and scurrying footsteps downstairs. I burrowed deeper into the hay.

Someone barked in German, "Do you hide Jews? Tell me? Where are they?" I heard heavy boots on the ladder leading to my hiding place.

"No," Mr. Swietlik said, just inches from my head. "There's no one here."

Just then I heard a muffled cry and a terrible commotion. When all was quiet again, the German voices were gone. I sat in the darkness, biting my fingernails until they bled. What had happened? What had saved me?

Some time later, Mr. Swietlik rapped on the wall, and I opened the trap door. His face was very red.

"Mother has had a heart attack," he said simply. When he saw the expression of horror on my face, he added, "Do not blame yourself, my child. She will recover."

I assumed they would send me away that very night, but, instead, they let me stay with them more than a month, until Christmas. I would have been better off on the road. I ate so many goodies over the holiday that I got violently ill. I was in so much pain that I was afraid I would die in their attic. Instead, I managed to climb down, say my goodbyes, and make my way to a nearby field.

For two days, I lay in the dirt, without food or water. My stomach felt as though someone were twisting it through Uncle Luzer's mangel.

At some point, I must have passed out, because when I came to, a woman was bending over me, patting my forehead and cheeks with a warm cloth. She brought me food, and when I could stand up, she helped me back home with her.

She told me that she had recognized me the moment she saw me. Her eldest son was a shoemaker, so they knew me from the store.

The family was very kind, but, as soon as I recovered, I had to move on. The children kept asking who I was, and I was afraid they would talk about me in the village.

So, cold as it was, I packed up my few belongings and headed back to the road. All of the Jews were gone now, which meant that no one came to look for them anymore. But still I had no place to stay. My only blessing was that now I could travel on the main roads from village to village without being seen. They were too icy for cars or horses.

At nightfall, I came to another village. As I trod through the streets, I saw a light in every house. Families huddled around their fires, their faces red and shiny. Harvest had passed, so parents had more time to sit with their little ones, making them toys, and telling stories. Even the dogs lay contentedly by the fire, warm and well fed.

There was no one alive in the world who was waiting for me, who looked forward to caring for me. The pain in my stomach was long gone. But the pain in my heart, I believed, would last forever.

# Leo

I wanted to kiss Andzia. I'm not going to beat around the bush or be coy about it. She was a beautiful girl, the most beautiful I ever saw. A regular *shayna madela,* as we say in Yiddish. The Song of Songs would've been written for Andzia if King Solomon had ever seen her!

I'd never kissed a girl before, but how hard could it be? I mean, it's just nature, isn't it? In Kanczuga, before we left the first time, my nonreligious friends and I would joke about this stuff. But we were kids then. What did we know about anything?

Now, I was a man. I'd worked like a man, supporting my sister while we were away. I read the papers. I was eighteen years old and completely on my own!

She came in one night to feed me, Andzia, wrapped in a bulky cloth coat, with a scarf and heavy boots. Outside, it was snowing, and, in the lantern light, the flakes melted on her nose and cheeks like dying stars. I wasn't cold at all, because the straw in my hiding place kept me pretty toasty. But she was chilled. She couldn't stop stamping her feet and hugging herself.

I thought, now that'd be a friendly gesture, to hold her and warm her up. I really don't think she would have minded. She had that way of tilting her head and smiling with her eyes half-closed, as I'd seen Faiga do to boys she liked. But something held me back. It wasn't that I wasn't good enough for her, even if I was just a Jew hiding in a box. But if Mr. Chmura found out or, God forbid, if he came in and saw us, I shuddered to think. The least he would do would be to keep her from coming back in. The most would be to throw me out. Either way I'd be a lot worse off than I was.

So instead, I dreamed about her, awake and asleep. There was no way I could ever marry Andzia, of course, but that little detail didn't make a difference to me. I pictured, as best I could, what we would do together when we were on our own. I dreamed about having her with me when the war was over and I returned to our house in Kanczuga. I wondered what people would say, seeing Luzer Rosenbluth striding back into town with Andzia Chmura on his arm. Now wouldn't that be something?

I told my mouse about her. About the odd little croaking sound she made when she laughed. The twinkle of her blue eyes when I made a funny face. The way her pink lips curved into a dimpled smile when she was pleased. The way she seemed to understand me, even though we could barely communicate in words. The looks she gave me when I was bending and running, as if she and I shared the same thoughts about each other. Or was I imagining that?

That night, when she couldn't get warm, I reached out my hands to take hers. Then I rubbed her sturdy pink fingers, one by one, over the lantern. Neither of us spoke. It was as if we both knew that this was the closest we could ever come to each other, that this was going to have to make up for all the other things that we would never be able to do.

I told Andzia that I'd read in the paper that the Russians were advancing, though I don't think she understood me. Sign language and lip-reading go only so far. Then I took out my mouse and let her pet it. I'd mentioned him before, but I'd been afraid to take him out in the open barn. Of course, he could have gotten out there any time, but I didn't want to tempt fate by taking him too near the door, even in winter. At first, she seemed to think it was pretty weird that I'd make such a big deal about a mouse. But, when she saw how tame it had become, and when I reminded her that I had no one else for twenty-two hours a day, I think she got the point.

She stayed longer than usual that night, long after she'd stopped shivering. And when she left, I climbed back in my cubbyhole. I felt empty and frustrated—and a whole lot better than I had in a long, long time.

# Fay

By the third summer, the roads were becoming more familiar. I was able to move from place to place with relative ease. The year was 1944, and most people in Poland had probably forgotten that Jews had ever existed. Still, I had to be on my guard. All it took was one angry peasant to stop me.

Sometimes people asked me, "What will happen to you when the war is over? Where will you go? Why don't you come back and marry one of our sons?"

I was amazed that people could be so kind. Thanking them for the offers, I said, "If I survive, I must remain Jewish and marry a Jew. That is who I am." I would then say that, as far as I knew, no one was left from my family. I was afraid to face my deep loneliness without them, but I knew I had a purpose in life. I must survive to tell the world what had happened to us.

One night, I was walking briskly in the direction of a village I knew well. I had been sitting all day, and now the trek was refreshing. The stars twinkled fiercely in the velvet sky, and a warm breeze ruffled the lush summer leaves, until the trees swayed like satin gowns on a thousand dancing princesses.

It was so late that a light was lit in just a single house. When I approached, dogs began to bark.

Just as I began to back off, someone opened the door and stepped into the darkness. Then another figure appeared.

My mind was racing, but my movements were slow as a snail. I slipped into the nearest wheat field and kept moving until I was standing roughly in the middle. Then I lay down, my ear close to the earth.

The two were soon joined by many others. I heard their voices above the rustle of the wind. One of them swore that he had seen me. He apparently had, because he accurately described what I looked like. Then someone said he was probably imagining the whole thing. Someone else said he had a machine gun.

For what seemed like hours, they combed the field, describing in loud, ugly tones what they would do if they found me. I longed to run, but I knew if I did I would be theirs.

I have no idea how I made it through that night. I did not dare to sob, or even to whisper a prayer, for fear of who would be close by. Never had I felt more like a hunted animal than I did that night. At one point, when the voices got close, I thought that I would wet myself with fear. I burrowed still deeper, inhaling the musky scent of soil mingled with that of my own fear.

Even if I could have slept, I did not dare. Who knew when I might turn over, or even snore, within hearing distance of my pursuers?

But even the longest nights draw to a close, and dawn rolls in with all the innocence of a new beginning. When I heard other voices, those of ordinary people going about their business, I stood up, stretched, and made my way out of the field. I was filthy and still shaking, but I was alive.

I knocked on only the doors I already knew. The peasants greeted me with surprise that I was still alive. One recommended me another. "Go there," they would say. "Not too many people are around." I never knew whom to trust, who would call the police and who would let me be.

I decided to make my way to Chodakówka, where I had some acquaintances. When I stopped at a village along the way, I saw a woman carrying a milking pail.

"Excuse me," I said. "Could you tell me the name of this village?"

When she told me, I almost fell over. People in that village were known for burying all their Jews themselves, saving the police the trouble.

I told her I wanted to go to Chodakówka, but I did not know the way.

"Stasiek, Stasiek!" she called out.

I looked around. A tall, good-looking boy lumbered toward us.

"Stasiek," she said to her son, "show her the shortcut to Chodakówka."

To me she added, "You have to go through the woods. When you get to the top of the hill, you will see the village."

The boy nodded and motioned to me to follow him. "Come on," he said with a strange smile, "let's get going."

I trembled. Five years ago, a healthy, handsome boy like that would

186

have aroused all my female instincts. But, that evening, all he did was terrify me.

Sure enough, as soon as we were out of sight of the road, he grabbed me. I tried to fight him, but his arms were the size of my thighs. He smelled of animals and sweat, and I caught the odor of his dinner on his breath as he tried to press his lips against mine.

"Stasiek," I said, as firmly as I could. "What pleasure is there to fight a poor, defenseless girl? I am hungry and dirty. There is no question who will win this battle. But what will you get out of it, except for a bad case of lice?"

He relaxed his grip a bit, and I wriggled away and fled deep into the forest. I did not hear him follow me, and I did not look back.

When I came to a clearing, I fell to my knees and wept for a long time.

At last I arrived in Chodakówka. As usual, I was turned away at door after door. I left the village and wandered into some of the more isolated houses off the road. Sometimes these people were lonely enough to welcome a visitor.

I came to a house that was new and still under construction. Building materials lay scattered on the ground like children's toys. A light burned in the window, so I knocked.

An older man came to the door, followed by a young woman. He asked what they could do for me.

"Could you let me stay here overnight?" I asked.

"Of course!" he answered, almost before the words were out of my mouth. "Come in and make yourself comfortable!"

During supper, they told me that he was a widower, and his companion was his girlfriend. After the meal, they started to undress. The man said that I could sleep in their bed with them.

"Thank you," I said, as politely as I could. "But if you don't mind, I will sleep in the straw."

He shrugged. "As you wish."

The next day, my hosts went off to town, first locking me in the house so I would be safe. I spent a lovely morning gazing out the window at the luxurious garden.

At noon, a horse and wagon stopped in front of the house. A young couple jumped out and tried the door. I knew it was locked, but I did not feel safe. I had just enough time to hide beneath the quilt on the bed before I heard them at the window. Then I heard the crash of broken glass.

As I lay breathless under the covers, they climbed up to the attic and came back down with a wagonload of hay.

When the widower came home, he sobbed like a baby. Then he went out to report the theft to the police, which meant that I had to be on my way. I consoled myself with the thought that it was a miracle I had not been spotted during the robbery.

It was not my worst brush with danger on the road, but it was the last that I could bear. Something inside of me gave way that day. I decided I had had enough. I could not hide another day. I would find work and live like any respectable peasant. And, if I could not, then I would die like the Jew that I was.

# Leo

I was reading the paper as usual, one letter at a time in my sliver of light. Suddenly I heard all this knocking and screaming! Then a low, gravelly voice cried out, "Żyd, Żyd!"

Hearing the Polish word for Jew, I almost lost it. My first thought was, Chmura gave me up. It was good while it lasted, but what could I expect? How could he put up with the danger for so long? It was almost a relief. At last, I thought, I will join my parents in the world to come.

When I listened to the voice again, I realized what had happened. It wasn't the police, but it still wasn't good. Mr. Chmura's simpleton son Tolek had finally spotted me.

Right outside my hiding place, I knew, were rabbit cages. Mr. Chmura thought this was a good idea, because the rabbit noise could drown out my noise. The wall was just pieces of lumber, with some knotholes. But we'd thought it would do the trick.

My mind was racing as fast as my heart. Tolek must've gone over to play with the rabbits and peeked through a hole I didn't even know about. Maybe he'd seen my foot. What did it matter? At last, the day I had waited for had arrived. Even if I was to be shot tomorrow, for a few hours, I would be free to walk outside.

I couldn't concentrate on the paper. I just kept thinking about the trip. How much food I should bring. Whether I should ask for money. For the first time since I'd been in hiding, I even thought of praying. But, when I tried, my prayers didn't get any further than the ceiling over my head. At last, I got some sleep, but it was the kind of sleep that was so twitchy and nervous, I felt even worse when I woke up.

When I heard Mr. Chmura's cough, I had the boards down almost before he'd closed the door.

"What happened out there today?" I asked.

189

At first, he looked confused. Then he said, "Oh, that! It was nothing."

I was stunned. "What do you mean?"

He settled down on a bundle of hay, stretching out his long legs. He said, "Tolek can say some words, but not many. He can't say 'rabbit,' but he can say 'Żyd.' One of the rabbits had babies today. It has kind of a beard, like a Jew. So, when he saw the baby rabbits, he called out 'Żyd.' Did the noise upset you?"

I stared at him for a second or two. When my heart finally settled back in my chest, I said, "Oh, no, not at all. I was just wondering."

# Fay

By now, everybody knew me in these villages, so I had to move further out. I walked all day, until I came to a charming little house on the edge of a village I had not been to before. I walked in without knocking and found a middle-aged woman leaning over the fire, stirring something in a big, black pot.

"Excuse me, ma'am," I said, as sweetly as I could. "Could you use some help? I'm much stronger than I look."

When the woman turned toward me, I saw that she was very ill. Her skin was yellow, and her eyes were dull.

At the sight of me, her face lit up. My heart warmed immediately. It had been a long time since anyone was happy to see me.

"Well, my dear, I can't pay you much," she began. "My husband passed away, God rest his soul, and my only son was sent to fight in Germany."

Briefly I told her my story, how my family was deported and I needed only a place to stay and some food to eat. The only part I left out was that I was Jewish.

She approached me and took hold of both my hands. "My child," she said, "you are a gift from God."

We sat down for supper, and then I undressed myself for the first time in many months and put on a simple shift the woman gave me to wear for bed. When she knelt to pray, I did the same, only I prayed in Hebrew. Then I settled down to sleep in the luxury of a real bed.

The woman's name was Angela. She was not very smart, and I was sure that she did not suspect anything. But her brother Anton and his family lived on the other side of the house. When we were introduced the next morning, I saw from the curl of his lips when he called me "Miss

191

Fela" that he knew exactly what, if not who, I was. Yet, to my great relief, he said nothing.

I worked for that family for several weeks, loading the filth from the sewer into a cart to be distributed in the field and garden. It was hard and foul-smelling work, but I was grateful to have it. I was especially glad when I had something to do in the garden, because it reminded me of our garden back home. Except, of course, that then I was a land-owner's daughter. A servant's view is somewhat different.

One day, a young man came to visit Anton. He spotted me before I saw him and rushed toward me.

"Is that you, Faiga?" he asked, his blue eyes sparkling with surprise.

I suddenly felt as though I would lose my breakfast. He was Stasiek, a shoemaker who had often visited our shop. Kind and handsome as he was, I still had every reason to fear him.

"Shhh!" I replied. "Here they know me as Fela."

I whisked past him and continued on to the house. Thank goodness, he did not call after me.

All day, I wondered what he and Anton were plotting. I caught sight of them from time to time, in the house or in the field, but they let me be. I figured it was only a matter of time before they made trouble for me.

But, the next day, Stasiek found me alone in the field. As he approached, a smile on his handsome face, I backed away.

"Don't be afraid!" he said, holding out his hands. "I won't hurt you! I just want to talk with you."

Where could I go, anyway? If he wanted to catch me, there was no stopping him. I stood where I was and waited for him to reach me.

"Don't worry," he said, taking my hand. "No one knows about you."

"Not even Anton?" I asked, pulling away my hand and hiding it behind my back.

He smiled at that. He said, "Anton hasn't said anything to me, and I'm his best friend."

"What do you want from me?"

"Only that you be careful. I will help you, if you want me to. The war is coming to an end, and then you'll be safe."

With my arms still behind my back, I asked, "How will you help me?"

"Let me be your boyfriend. Then no one will dare to come near you."

I sighed. Not so long ago, I would have jumped at the chance to be in this young man's company. He had good manners. He was as kind and good-looking as anyone I had ever known.

"You have to understand," I said, "I am fighting for my life here. And, besides, look at me. I am not exactly feeling womanly, if you know what I mean."

I felt him study my dirty face and hair, the grit beneath my fingernails and the stains on my clothing. He said, "I still think you're beautiful. But I can wait until you're ready. In the meantime, Faiga—"

"I am not Faiga anymore," I interrupted him. "I am Fela. Remember, that's what I told them!"

"Fela, Fela. I'm sorry. Look, I ask nothing of you. I swear that not even my own mother will find out about you. I only want to help you."

"What do you ask from me in return?" I repeated.

He sighed. "I ask only that you be careful. I will help you, if you want me to. You don't have much longer to hold out. The Russians will be here any day to take this country back from the Germans. Then you'll be safe."

He came to see me many times over the next weeks. I cleaned myself up as best I could, not so much to attract him as not to be repulsive. In the evenings, we strolled and talked for hours, and I came to rely on his clever conversation and kindness. When he held me, I sighed with pleasure.

But then I started hearing whispers in the village about me. Or maybe they were the rattlings in my own head, which had never recovered from my attack. It did not matter. Much as it hurt to tear myself away from Stasiek and this comfortable place, it was time to move on. Besides, I knew I could never marry a goy. My parents would die a second death, if such a thing were possible.

I hesitated as long as I could. Then one day, I was working at the potato field and came home for lunch. There, sitting at the table, was one of the most handsome men from our town, someone my friends and I had gossiped about for years. He knew me immediately but did not say a word. I was so upset that I excused myself from the table and returned to the fields to think.

Now I knew I had no choice. I said goodbye to Angela and Anton and hugged Stasiek with all the strength I could muster. When I returned to the road, it was with a heart brimming with longing.

# Leo

Andzia told me she was sorry that I had to stay cooped up all the time. Her face turned red, and tears splashed down her cheeks, real soft, like rain in summertime. She made me feel like some kind of hero. Lonek the Brave!

"Be strong, Lonek!" she said. "It won't be much longer!"

When she said that, I thought, maybe little Luzer Rosenbluth, with the payos hanging from his ears and the black satin coat, couldn't have held out so long. But Lonek the Brave can do anything. Lonek the Brave! Lonek the Bold! Lonek the Undefeatable! Hater of Hitler, Defender of the Jews!

One night she brought me geraniums. I never heard of a girl giving a boy flowers, but they say that in wartime, the world turns upside down.

"There is so much beauty outside in my world," she said. "I wanted to bring some of it to yours."

I thanked her for the flowers, but you want to know the truth? She brought beauty every time she came to see me.

All that night, I lay awake thinking about Andzia. I was trying to figure out whether it was all right to marry a shiksa if there were no other Jews left in the world. It seemed fair to me, but I wasn't so sure what our rabbi would say.

When I heard Mr. C.'s cough the next evening, I was a little disappointed. I had hoped to get another visit from my flower girl. But then I saw his face, and I forgot about Andzia in a minute. He looked like a crazy person. His cheeks were red, and his eyes were feverish.

"What is it?" I asked, as he practically danced toward me and grabbed hold of my shoulders. "What's happened?"

"I have a feeling that this time the Germans are on their way out," he said. "I was in Kanczuga this morning. People told me that the war is almost over. I even saw a few Jews!"

His voice, usually a low whisper, was now almost a shout. I guess he no longer cared who heard him. But I needed more evidence.

"Is it the truth?" I murmured, my voice shaking. "Or is this one of your stories to make me hold on a little longer?"

He frowned and said, "I don't tell you stories. But I want to go back again tomorrow, to make sure. Just to get another look around."

All the next day, I waited for him, trying not to think. About anything. That night, Mr. Chmura came into the barn without giving his special signal.

"We did it!" he said, reaching out to give me a hug. "You can go home now! You're safe!"

Then he handed me a covered plate, saying, "I've brought you some of Mother's stew to celebrate!"

It was strange, I know, but my first thought, after two years in his barn, was not about celebration. All I could think of was how badly he wanted me out of there. How hard it must have been for him. But then I felt pretty stupid. This man had saved my life. He had cared for me unselfishly. How could I not be happy that I was free?

"So," I said, staring down at the greasy cubes of meat. "I guess I should go back to Kanczuga then."

"Of course. You'll want to see whether your sister is alive, won't you? And you'll want to reclaim your home."

That's when I lay down my spoon.

"What is it?" he asked. "Are you ill?"

"No," I said, setting down the plate at my feet. "I'm fine. It's great. I just—I'm scared. I feel like an idiot for saying this, but I'm scared. Those people—how are they going to treat us?"

"Kanczuga is your home," he said. "The Germans are gone now. And your parents were respected by everyone. They have no right to treat you with anything but respect."

I sighed. "Yet look what happened."

Mr. Chmura leaned over and clapped a hand on my shoulder.

"Hey," he said, "I was so excited for you that I didn't stop to think how hard this would be. Of course you're nervous. Stay here as long as you like."

I thought of the hiding place. The long hours of blackness. Reading by

195

pinhole, my best friend a field mouse. I thought of the way my guts had turned to jelly when I heard the word *Żyd*.

I shook my head. "If I'm a free man," I said, "I should live like one. You and your family have been great to me. And don't worry. One day soon, I will repay you for saving my life."

"We didn't do it for payment, son."

"I know that, but you deserve everything I have. I owe everything to you. You and—"

He smiled. "Would you like to say goodbye to Andzia before you leave?"

I tried to sound as if I didn't care. "Sure," I said. "If that'd be okay."

"I'll go get her. In the meantime, I have something for you." He handed me a package with some food and a little money. "This is to get you started," he said. "Tell you what. If you want, you can repay me for this."

"I don't know how to thank you," I said. My hands were shaking as I reached for the money.

His eyes filled with tears. "Your life is thanks enough, my son."

A few minutes after he left, Andzia came to the door. She handed me a picture of herself and turned it over to show what she'd written on the back: "If you remember, keep it. If you forget, throw it away."

We held each other for a long time. Then I kissed her, right on the lips. And then I walked back into the world.

# Fay

I hardly knew where I was headed, but somehow my feet found the way back to Siedlecka, a village I knew well. I knocked on the door of a shoemaker whose mother was a legend among the Jews of my town. She was the only Jew in our history who had converted to Catholicism.

The family welcomed me like a long-lost relative. They insisted that I not hide, but rather live with them as one of their daughters, who were about my age. I spent my days knitting sweaters and helping with the housework. I was happy there and should have been more content than anywhere else in my travels. But something kept gnawing at me, some unsettling feeling that I could not name.

Then, one day, my hostess came home from the market so excited that she grabbed me before the door had even swung shut. When she had caught her breath, she said, "The Russians have returned. You are free!"

I considered. I was delighted that the Nazis were gone, but I had no idea what it would mean for me. Life under the Russian occupation had been almost as dangerous as it was under the Germans.

Before I could say anything, she blurted out, "I have something else to tell you, my dear!" Her grin was as bright as a candle flame. She said, "I saw a boy in town today who looks just like you. You have to go back to Kanczuga and find out whether it's your brother!"

No words could express the range of emotions I felt. For two years, I had lived a life that was not my own. Now it was time to pick up where mine had left off. I prayed that my brother would be there to share it with me.

# Leo

Dazed and numb, that's how I felt walking through the familiar streets. Right away I saw several of my father's customers. Just like the last time I came home, they walked right past me. Children stared at me from doorways like I was an escaped convict.

Everything looked the same—except there were no more Jews. I couldn't help thinking of other times I'd walked these streets. I remembered listening to the nigunim the Jewish families sang around the Shabbos table. I thought of one time when a black man came to town in a little sports car, the first automobile I'd ever seen. He was a seven-foot-tall American, handing out free samples of coffee. I ran around yelling my head off for everybody to come see.

The first Jew I saw was Willie Kromberg, who had hidden with a family, too. How many centuries ago was it we played jacks and built a wagon? We hugged, and then we punched each other. Guys have to punch each other, especially if they first hug each other like a couple of girls. We both had whiskers now, and our voices were lower. It was as if we were different people.

Then Willie told me that he thought he had seen Faiga, and for a minute I almost broke down. That's all I needed, for Willie Kromberg to see me crying on my first day back.

We wandered the streets, Willie looking for other Jews, me for my sister. We met a couple of friends who had come back from a work camp, where they had manufactured ammunition. It seemed that everybody who had survived was about my age, and almost all of them were boys. But Willie said that more Jews were coming back to town all the time.

We talked that day like the closest of brothers. Hour after hour, we discussed what it was like for us in hiding, what we had heard about this one and that. Neither of us mentioned Faiga. It was understood that the subject was off limits.

When it started to get dark, he took me to one of the few houses in town where he said all the survivors were staying. I asked him why I couldn't just go back to my own house, and he looked at me kind of funny.

"It's not your house anymore, kid," he said.

I shook my head. "What are you talking about?"

But that was all he said. We joined a bunch of survivors, people our age, and ate a simple meal together in a house not far from mine. When I bedded down on the floor that night, I thought I would never fall asleep. I had seen more that day than I had in the past two years put together, and I thought my head would just about explode from all the excitement. Instead, it shut down from exhaustion. I was asleep in no time.

When I opened my eyes the next morning, I didn't know where I was. I felt a panic that didn't go away for a long time. Even the sight of Willie and the others didn't help. I got up and ate some bread as quick as I could, then ran off into the streets again.

Willie had warned me not to, but still I found myself circling around the Kolejova, sort of homing in on our house. I knew the Kwasniaks would be inside. How could it hurt to see them? We grew up with them, went to school with their kids. Why wouldn't they welcome me?

I turned the corner to our street. And that's when I saw my sister. She was very thin, and, with her messed-up hair and frayed dress, she looked like a doll that had dropped on the floor and rolled into a corner. Cracked and dusky, but still beautiful.

She must've seen me first, because she was already running in my direction, while I could only stand still in surprise. When we held each other, the tears poured down our faces, and when we kissed each other's cheeks, I could taste our weeping. I was afraid to hug her too hard. I thought of my mouse, back in Chmura's barn.

She said, "You look wonderful! As healthy as a fatted calf!"

"I wish I could say the same about you."

"Let's go someplace where we can talk."

But there was nowhere for us to be alone, so we walked all over town, hardly noticing where we went, just talking and talking. I kept reaching out to her. I couldn't let go of her hand, couldn't stop touching her hair, just to convince myself this wasn't a dream. As she told me her story, I was glad to know it was our parents' goodness that had helped us both survive.

When I said I'd been with the Chmuras in Siedlecka, her tanned face turned pale.

"What is it?" I asked, stopping in the middle of the street.

"It's just that—" She shook her head in disbelief. "I was in Siedlecka much of the time. We were so close, but we never knew!"

We decided to try our luck with the Kwasniaks at our house. At first I was a little nervous, I admit. But then Faiga told me how Rózia had helped her, so I felt better about it. When we got to the house, I reached for the doorknob.

"Wait!" she said, taking hold of my arm. "You can't just walk in like that! This isn't our house anymore."

I nodded and knocked, a funny feeling in the pit of my stomach.

Rózia came to the door. I couldn't figure out what was different about her, why she was so familiar and yet so strange.

She seemed happy to see us and invited us inside. They'd moved a few things around, but the house looked pretty much the same. Then I got it. What had changed was Rózia's manner. Before she was the servant; now she was the lady of the house. I saw right away that Willie was right. She treated us like guests, honored guests, maybe, but not the rightful owners. Still, there was something nagging at me.

When it was time to go to sleep, she made up beds for us in the attic, where they hung the clothes to dry. They threw down some straw on the floor for us, and we were pretty comfortable, considering where we'd slept for the past two years.

As we lay side by side, I whispered to Faiga, "What is it about her?"

"Don't you know?" she hissed back. "She's wearing Mamche's things!"

At that, the funny feeling in my stomach became a slow burn.

We stayed a week or two. But it was obvious that we were just temporary boarders. And, with Kwasniak's history of ratting on us, we knew he didn't want us around. Afraid we would be murdered in our sleep, we started taking turns as lookouts.

Tata had hidden some stuff in the cellar, money and a silver candlestick, in case any of us came back after the war. On one of the few afternoons when we were alone in the house, we looked for them. No luck. After a couple of hours, we climbed out of the cellar, filthy and aggravated. The Kwasniaks had gotten there first.

Then Faiga started to have these nightmares. She was so afraid that the Kwasniaks would kill us that she never fell asleep for more than a few minutes at a time. We figured we couldn't take any more chances.

200

# Fay

It wasn't long before we found a place to live with other survivors. Despite all the sadness and ghosts that surrounded us, I could not feel sad. We were embarking on a new life, Luzer and I. Only a couple of dozen Jews had returned to Kanczuga. Yankele Kelstecher, who had hidden for a while in the monument called Kapliczka after jumping off the wagon bound for the cemetery. Yehuda Ehrlich. Sidney Silverman, a very tall, good-looking friend my age. Nathan Shifman, an acquaintance. Toni Laufer, who had been several years ahead of me in school. A few older people. Of all of us, Luzer and I were the only two from the same family. I was amazed at how lucky we were, and how kind were the people who had helped us.

Adding to my happiness, not long after arriving in Kanczuga, I began keeping company with a young man named Azriel Reizfeld. He had been working in Stalowa Wola. He was a dentist, an accomplished musician with high spirits and a wonderful sense of humor. And, unlike most of the town's Jews, he was able to return to his own house.

Izzy and I took long walks during the day and spent every evening together. I felt young and hopeful again, happier than I had been in years. After a month or so, he asked me to marry him. In the meantime, he said, he wanted Luzer and me to come and live with him.

I went back to the house where I was staying with my brother and told him about the proposal.

"Do you love him?" he asked.

I could not answer him, and I put off giving Izzy an answer, as well. Although he asked me every day, I refused to move in with him. In that town, a religious girl could never get away with such a thing, even with her brother along as chaperon. Proud as I was, I would not even take his sister's clothing that was hanging in his closets.

Meanwhile, two beautiful cousins we knew returned from hiding. Izzy told me about them, and together we set out to make them feel welcome.

It was certainly more than the Gentiles did for them. I was growing more and more fearful of our neighbors. The whole town was like one big cemetery, with Jewish graves in many yards. Wherever we went, we were greeted by sneers and whispers. One night, I was visiting Jewish friends when someone tossed a grenade through the window. Thank goodness, it did not go off.

If it had not been for Izzy's constant attention, I would have been even more afraid. Being married to Izzy would make me feel secure, I knew. And he was so kind and attentive. I did not discount marriage with him; I was just not ready.

Not long after the cousins arrived, I realized that I had not seen Izzy for two days. This was not like him, and I worried that something had happened to him. I got up early and set off for his house. Without knocking, I opened the front door. In an instant, I took in the scene: one of those gorgeous cousins asleep in Izzy's bed, and Izzy in the kitchen making breakfast.

I tiptoed out without being seen. Then I ran all the way home.

"Luzer!" I cried, arriving breathless at the house.

He looked up from his newspaper. "What is it?"

"Luzer, this is no place for us. You'll never believe what I saw!"

We left the next morning. On our way out of town, we stopped off at the cemetery to say goodbye to our parents and sisters, who lay with hundreds of others in a huge, hastily covered pit. Luzer told me what Mamche had said before leaving him, how she wanted us to lead good Jewish lives. I gazed at the ragged mound of earth and wept. So this was it, the sum total of hundreds of generations of faith in God. This was where it ended.

Like thieves, my brother and I crept out of the place where we were born, where the best parts of ourselves lay buried beneath the earth. We did not know then how lucky we were to go. Two weeks later, Izzy and the cousins were murdered, shot in his house along with other Jews who had recently come home.

# Leo

We slept overnight in Przeworsk, then moved on to Przemyśl, which was now completely under Russian control. It was mid-October 1944. The Russians were still fighting the Nazis. We heard they were looking for young men to draft into the army. Faiga made me hide in the two-room flat we shared with a guy named Wolf Singer and some other survivors. She went out every day to the black market to try to make a few złotys to buy us bread.

But I'd been cooped up for two years! I had to go outside, just to breathe the fresh air and to feel the sunshine on my papery skin.

A week or two after we arrived, I was standing around with a few people in front of our building when three soldiers came over to us, saying they wanted us to join the Russian army.

"I'm Polish," I said. "We already fought the Nazis."

One of the officers took a menacing step toward me. He said, "Didn't Hitler hurt your family? Don't you want to get your revenge?"

I shook my head. "Not that way."

I guess I didn't convince them. They dragged us to their headquarters, where they threw us in a room with a lot of other men our age. Then they shaved off our hair.

Through it all, I tried to reason with them. I said, "But I don't know how to shoot a gun! I'd be a terrible soldier!"

"Don't worry," one of them said. "We'll teach you how."

When the officer left, one of the soldiers whispered to me, "They don't care if you can't fight. You'll never have a chance to shoot a gun."

"What are you talking about?"

He looked around to see if anyone was listening. Then he said, "You're going to be sent to the minefields, as human minesweepers. They used to use criminals from the prisons for this duty instead of executing them."

A chill went right through me. Here I'd survived in a barn, only to be killed in a minefield. I had twenty-four hours to come up with a plan. My first worry was my hair. When people saw you had no hair, they knew right away you were a deserter. Somehow I found a little gray cap, with a brim. That solved half my problem. Now, all I needed to do was escape. But how to do that, I had no idea. It looked as if all the care that had gone into saving my life was about to be for nothing.

# Fay

As soon as I walked in the door, I knew something was wrong. The house was silent as a grave, and none of my roommates could look me in the eyes. When they told me that soldiers had taken Luzer, I became frantic. Oh God, I thought, will you never stop testing us?

I gathered together the little money we had made on the black market, along with my sole possession of any value, a watch. The only information the survivors could give me about his whereabouts was that they had gone in the direction of the old prison. I set off at a run. I cannot imagine what the people in the street must have thought of me, dashing through the city, tears streaming down my face, mumbling over and over, "God help me find him; that's all I have, my brother!"

When I reached the prison, I beat my fists on the heavy iron door. For a long time, nothing happened. Then a tall Russian soldier appeared and pushed me away with long, cold fingers.

"What are you doing here?" he barked. "This is a prison! Go away!"

All I could do was weep. It worked. He let me in.

Right away, I saw my brother and his friends in the midst of a group of young men. When our eyes met, he started to cry, too. The guard who had opened the door casually mentioned that the men would be moving soon, but no one knew where.

It doesn't matter, I told myself. Wherever they go, I will follow.

A second guard came in and led the young men to another room for a lecture. I was alone with the man who had opened the door. I knew something about bribing Russians. Dangerous as it could be, it was my only chance to secure my brother's freedom.

I looked up into pale blue eyes that were fierce with hatred. He smiled back at me, but it was a cynical smile, brimming with contempt.

Before I had a chance to open my mouth, the young men were being led out of the lecture room and toward the door. When I started to follow, the guard blocked my way.

As discreetly as I could, I unhooked my watch and handed it to him.

"Please, sir," I said. "Please help my brother escape. He is all I have."

The man took the watch and leered down at me, saying, "If he tries, he will be shot on the spot."

"But sir," I persisted. "You could make sure he is not seen."

Through all of this, I felt my brother's eyes on me. I did not dare return his gaze.

The soldier's face grew red. He grabbed hold of me and dragged me into one of the filthy little cells. Ignoring my screams, he locked me in and disappeared.

I heard a commotion and raced to the cell's tiny window. There I saw the group being taken away. I screamed, I banged on the door, but no one came for me.

I do not know how long it took, but, at last, hungry and exhausted, I crumbled into a heap and fell asleep on the icy floor.

Suddenly the door opened with a bang, and a group of soldiers came in. Their immense chests were pinned with medals of every color of the rainbow.

"Get up!" one of them said gruffly. "Come with us."

I found myself in a large room that seemed to be a courtroom. After a minute or two, an elderly officer with slicked-back white hair and kind eyes entered and took his seat behind the table. Motioning to the other chair, he told me to sit down.

My hair was a mess, and my face and hands were filthy. I must have looked like the poorest of beggars, which was not very far from the truth. While the old man and his officers discussed my case, I tried to flatten my hair with my fingers.

One of them approached me. In perfect Polish, he snarled, "This is a military court. You are on trial for bribing a Russian soldier. Because we are at war, you could be sentenced to death."

If only I could have told them what I was doing there! But I was not allowed to speak.

"Just answer the questions," the Polish-speaking officer told me. "Are you related to Luzer Rosenbluth?"

I told him that I was. In answer to his questions, I said that I was his sister and that he was only sixteen.

"That's impossible," they told me. "The boy is not sixteen."

"But I'm telling the truth!" I said, trying to believe the lie myself. "I am twenty-one, and he is five years younger."

"Just answer the questions, little miss. You know," he added, "the war is not over. Our soldiers are dying every day, and the Jews must help us fight Hitler, not hide in their homes. What you did is punishable by firing squad."

He held up my watch and said, "Is this yours?"

I nodded. "Yes, sir."

There was more conferring. Then he said, "My associate recommends that I send you to Siberia to work for the rest of your life. But I will not do that. I shall take into consideration that you have lost your family, and therefore I am letting you go free. Do you have anything to say to the court?"

"My fate is in your hands," I said, bowing my head. "But, please, have mercy on my brother. Don't separate us."

"I'm sorry," he said, shaking his head. "There is nothing I can do for him. Now go home, and be sure that you never break the law again."

I was released. When I stepped outside, the sun shone down on me like a searchlight. I was as lost and alone as I had ever been in my life.

The once-elegant streets of Przemyśl were teeming with refugees from the war, their tragedies written on their gaunt faces. But no one, I was sure, looked as desperate as I. Whomever I passed, I asked whether they had seen a column of prisoners. At last, an old man said he had seen them marching in the direction of the railroad station.

I flew to the station, where I learned what train the men had taken. Then I boarded the next train going in that direction and roamed the packed cars, asking whether anyone had any idea where soldiers might be taken. A woman called out that her village had a recruiting camp operating in an old prison.

It was my best hope. I got out at the desolate train depot, with no idea how to proceed. When I started to walk, I was filled with an indescribable grief. Left, right, left, right. Here I was again, friendless and alone on a country road. I had thought that those days were gone forever. The only difference was that, instead of fearing for my own life, I was afraid for that of my brother.

After a while, some farmers passed by on a wagon, and I asked them which way to the prison. They pointed straight ahead, but before I could request a ride, they had passed me by.

By the time I reached the huge gates, I was shaking with fear and exhaustion. A watchman stood out front, a square-jawed fireplug of a man with a perpetual sneer. I begged him to let me in, but he said it was against orders.

And then, as if by a miracle, the young men poured out of the gate. I gasped when I saw Luzer. He ran to me, and we embraced. Then he said, "The front is only a few miles away. We leave in a day or two. Quick, get your hands on some whiskey and tobacco. We're going to try to escape."

And then he was gone. The sky was growing dark, and my legs would not carry me much farther. I came upon a farmhouse and asked where I could buy some whiskey and tobacco. They pointed to a deserted-looking building down the road. I pulled out my bills, so many, thanks to inflation, that I had tied them in a bundle with string. I bought the supplies and managed to deliver them to my brother. It was already quite late when I returned to the farmhouse and collapsed on a bed of straw on the floor. But, tired as I was, I doubt that my eyes ever shut. At first light, I jumped up and returned to the iron gates.

When he saw me, the watchman said, "They're not here anymore. And don't ask me where they went. I have no idea."

I was too frantic to cry. A car approached, a big Russian model. I flagged it down, and the officers inside gave me a ride into town. One of them I recognized from my trial, but we pretended not to know each other. Or maybe he truly did not know me. To him, I was probably just one more hard luck story.

When I was dropped off in front of our communal house in Przemyśl, I almost could not go in. How would I face the survivors inside, when my brother was not among them?

To my surprise, I was greeted by warm embraces and smiles. What could be worth celebrating at a time like this? Then someone handed me a telegram. My brother and his friends had escaped and were hiding in a neighboring village. I later learned that he had asked the watchman to let him go outside to relieve himself. In the compound, he had given the man the tobacco and whiskey in exchange for his agreement to look the other way while Luzer and the others scaled the prison wall. They had then walked all night until they found a house where they could hide.

When I saw my brother's name at the bottom of the page, I fell to my knees and sobbed. Then I gathered a few things and set out once more to the station.

He was waiting for me when I got off the train. Neither of us said a word. We just stood in the midst of the crowd and held each other.

# Leo

Now I was on the run. We made up our minds to take the train to Lublin, where a lot of survivors had gathered after it was liberated by the Russians. Lublin was a pretty good-size city, and we were hoping to disappear among the faces.

Lublin was on the Bystrzyca River, maybe a hundred miles southeast of Warsaw. It'd been a trading city since the tenth century and was known for its ancient citadel, a sixteenth-century cathedral, and a university. For Jews, Lublin had been a center of learning for generations. During the war, there was a Jewish ghetto there and four subcamps of Majdanek, where prisoners worked as forced laborers. The city had housed the headquarters of Operation Reinhard, the plan to kill the Jews of central and southern Poland.

The local Jewish council put us up in a refugee shelter, which was just a fancy name for a two-room flat in a lousy part of town. They had a soup kitchen, and we could stay as long as we wanted. But the soup was not much more than colored water, and we were told that there wasn't always enough to go around. New arrivals were coming every day from the camps, walking skeletons with that glazed-over look in their eyes, as if they'd seen the face of the devil. They stretched out on the floor at night, and many of them never made it back up in the morning.

It was summer, and the warm air was thick with sickness and death. The place was noisy and uncomfortable, not to mention swarming with lice. After the first horrible night, I went with the two fellows who had escaped from prison with me to find us all a place to live. We knocked on every door we came to; then we asked people in the marketplace. Finally, we met a nice woman about my mother's age who said she'd give us a room. It was clean and warm, and we agreed right away. The whole place was only one bedroom and a kitchen, but this woman said she and her kids would take the kitchen. We slept on mattresses in the other room.

We thought she was nice and friendly, and that was about all. But it wasn't long before we realized that she had an awful lot of male visitors. Faiga and I didn't get it at first, but one of my friends explained that we were living with a prostitute. Every time she had a client, we all had to troop outside. To say it was depressing is an understatement. We felt we had reached a new low.

# Fay

I was troubled by our arrangement in Lublin. Besides the fact that our parents would have been shocked by where we were living, winter was fast approaching. We had no warm clothing, which made it hard to go outside whenever our landlady had a customer. And, despite the fact that the war had turned in the Allies' favor, peace was as elusive as ever.

I sat at the table by the apartment window, gazing out at the grim city. On the street, I wandered without a purpose, looking inward more than out, wondering where to go, what to do.

One afternoon, a car stopped in front of me, disturbing my reverie and almost knocking me down.

A dark-haired, elegant Russian officer rolled down the back window. He said, "Excuse me, miss, do you know if there are any Jews in this town?"

"I am Jewish," I said, staring into the mesmerizing blue eyes. As soon as the words were out of my mouth, I wondered if I should have been more careful. Kanczuga wasn't the only place where Jews were being killed after liberation.

The officer broke into a delighted smile. "That's wonderful," he said. "So am I. Where are you from?"

When I told him, he said we were neighbors, because he was originally from Przemyśl. He said his father had a cousin in Kanczuga.

"Really?" I asked. He spoke in a haughty manner, and I had the sense that he was looking down on me, even though he was the one seated in the car. Nevertheless, I could feel my excitement mounting as I asked, "Who?"

Without a moment's hesitation, he uttered the name that was most deeply embedded in my heart. He said, "Balci Rosenbluth. Do you know her?"

If Captain Mayer Langsam had not been my mother's cousin's son,

211

perhaps we would not have connected so fiercely. But a spark ignited between us at that first meeting, and it grew more intense with each passing day. Mayer was unlike anyone I had ever seen. He was so wealthy that, when he pulled his handkerchief from his pocket, a stack of bills fell onto the ground. Yet he was also down-to-earth and genuine. He took me out to have our pictures taken the day after we met. He bought food for all our friends. He told me stories of his experiences and listened intently to mine. We reminisced about our family.

I soon fell in love with him, but what could he possibly see in me, a poor refugee? We sat holding hands for hours at a time, yet he never embraced me, never kissed me in more than a friendly way befitting a cousin. I longed for him to be more physical, but I was a well-brought-up young woman, and being forward was out of the question.

One day, Mayer invited me out for a drive. He said he was going to Berlin, that a major battle was expected there the following week.

"We are having an officers' ball," he told me. "I want you to come."

I shrank back in the luxurious leather seat. "Me? At an officers' ball?" I pointed to my frayed hem and soiled shoes. I said, "Look how shabby I am! I couldn't be seen at a ball!"

"You're my girl," he replied. "I want you to be there."

I was adamant. He offered to buy me a dress, but my pride would not allow it. We parted soon after, with his usual gentlemanly peck on the cheek.

Every day, I pored over the papers for news of the battle of Berlin. It was a terrible conflagration. With each passing day, I was more sure that Mayer could never survive it. I was surprised to find that my heart, shattered so many times over the years, was still capable of such agony. I was in love with Mayer Langsam, but I had not told him. How could I, when he treated me like a young cousin? And now I might never see him again. I prayed for him. I wrote "Berlin" again and again on scraps of paper, as if to keep the city safe with a magic spell.

Meanwhile, Kraków was liberated, and Luzer and I went there to live out the war. It was the largest city we had ever seen, more than five hundred years old, with huge buildings, a university where the astronomer Copernicus had studied, and a Gothic cathedral from the fourteenth century. Of course, it was the thriving black market that most interested us. My brother started to earn some money, and I was able to make us some decent clothing. Once again, Wolf Singer, who had arrived earlier, opened up his apartment to us. For the first time, Luzer and I had our own bedrooms. We made good friends. We even discovered a distant cousin, and she and her family came to live with us.

I reunited with a survivor from Kanczuga, Joseph Walker, who had spent much of his life in Berlin. We began to keep company. He was a gentle man, fourteen years older than I, handsome and quiet, with a kind heart.

Like most survivors I knew, I was hungry to marry and raise a family. But I knew what it was to be in love. Love was how I'd felt about Mayer Langsam, and I did not possess those feelings for Joe. One evening, I told him how it was and suggested that he stop visiting me. When he returned the very next day, I left the house. Instead of getting the idea, he called for me again.

He took me to a small cafe and proposed to me. I hesitated, but only for a few seconds. He was a good man. I was lonely. There was no one else in my life.

Joe and I announced our engagement the day the war ended, as a sign of hope for the future. But, apart from our impending marriage, we felt we had precious little to celebrate. We had lost our families, our home, our security, and more than five years of our lives. My hearing was very poor as a result of the blow I received in Schodnica, and what I did hear was marred by the constant ringing in my head.

Nevertheless, our days were filled with happiness. Since the liberation, we had been surviving; now we were thriving. We went swimming and out to nightclubs, and Luzer bought me jewelry. Joe gave me a fox stole. Despite my material comfort, I thought of my family all the time, and always my thoughts turned to Mayer. My love for him had grown stronger in the year since we had said goodbye. His dazzling eyes and serious manner filled my dreams. I was sad to think that that chapter of my life was closed forever.

Then, one day late in August 1945, Luzer burst into the apartment.

"What is it?" I asked, looking up from the dishes I had been washing in the sink.

"He's back," he said simply.

He did not have to say more. All at once, I felt so dizzy, I moved to the table and sat down.

"What—?" I asked. "When—?"

"He's coming tomorrow," Luzer said, avoiding my gaze.

How to spend the few hours until I would see Mayer again? Should I have my hair done? But then what was I doing, primping for my cousin?

213

When I heard his knock, I was glad that Joe was away on business. I jumped up and opened the door, and Mayer fell into my arms, Mayer my love, whom I had prayed for every night we were apart.

Except for being in civilian clothes, he looked almost the same, as if he had never been through the torment of Berlin. Only his eyes looked sadder, but they crinkled with delight when he looked at me.

Before I could get past "hello," he was babbling like a madman. "I loaded a truck full of things, beautiful things for us in Berlin," he said, his words tumbling one on top of the next. "I rented the perfect apartment for us in Warsaw. I can't wait to show it to you! You have no idea how hard I've looked for you. I went to every city with Jews in it, trying to track you down!"

My face must have expressed my dismay, because he added quickly, "I know it was foolish. I haven't even asked you to marry me yet. But you were what kept me going during that terrible time in Berlin. It was your face I saw every day. It was your safety I prayed for every night."

"But—but—" I stammered. "You didn't tell me. I never knew how you felt!"

He hung his head. "I know. I didn't want you to grieve for me if I didn't make it. But that's all over with," he said brightly. "Now that we're together, I can tell you that I love you, that I've always loved you."

My mouth was dry. Once again, the room began to spin.

"What is it?" he asked. "Don't you love me?"

I wanted to shake him. I wanted to strike him across that handsome face. Instead, I struggled to get the words out.

"Oh, Mayer," I said, my voice breaking with anguish. "I love you with all my heart. But I'm married. Two weeks ago."

I thought of the simple ceremony. I had worn a short dress and a sort of crown in my hair, because we could not afford a veil. Joe had an old suit that a tailor had somehow revitalized by ripping apart and turning inside out. Luzer had been at my side, along with many new and old friends, who had bought flowers and helped me prepare food.

It had not been the wedding I had always imagined. No music, no dancing, not a single member of my family apart from my brother. At the appropriate time, Joe and I sipped a bit of wine. When he shattered the glass on the floor in the traditional Jewish way, the sound exploded in my weakened ears. I like to think it was loud enough to be heard back in the graveyard in Kanczuga.

Before Mayer could respond, I said, "I didn't know. I had no idea that you felt the same way about me as I did about you. I didn't even want to marry Joe. I just didn't know."

Mayer stayed in town a few days, until Joe's return. My love took us to a cafe, where he told my new husband to take good care of me. It was not an idle remark. Jews were being murdered all over the city. Then Mayer gave me his picture, the one taken a year earlier. On the back, he wrote, "I'm sorry I didn't tell you."

I introduced Mayer to a good friend. She was a lovely woman about my age. They were soon engaged, and I decided to make them an engagement party. The Sunday of the party arrived, but Mayer never appeared. My friend was hysterical, accusing him of deserting her.

We rushed to the hotel where he was staying with his adjutant.

"He never got over you," she said on the way. "I should have known by how he looked at you. He never wanted to marry me."

Maybe I was secretly pleased, but at the same time my heart was breaking for my friend. Meanwhile, I tried to suppress another thought: Jews were disappearing all the time.

"He is an honorable man," I told her, taking her arm in mine. "He wouldn't walk out on you. You've got to trust him! Something must have come up."

"I will never forgive him," she replied. "Not if I live a hundred years."

By the time we reached the hotel, she had calmed down a bit. We raced up to his room. The bed was unmade; clothing still hung in the closet. Mayer's adjutant, a young Polish boy, said he had not returned to the hotel the previous night.

His body was never found.

Mayer's disappearance left a hole in my heart. We were afraid to stay in Kraków; we wanted to get away from Europe altogether and never look back. I had always wanted to make *aliyah* to Palestine, but we knew that life was dangerous there, and we wanted, at long last, to be safe. We registered to emigrate to the United States and were told it would take time to get a visa. Then we heard that Jews were going to Germany, which at least was in the right direction. We had a connection with some Polish soldiers—everybody did at that time—who agreed to smuggle us out. One night, a good friend from Kanczuga, my husband, and I climbed into the bed of a military truck and covered ourselves with blankets and uniforms. Luzer went separately, in case something happened to us. Before we left, we put all our money in a valise, loosening the cardboard bottom and then replacing it over the bills. We gave it to a

Jewish officer who was able to travel by train. He agreed to deliver it to a friend of ours near Munich, where we would retrieve it.

After a couple of hours, we climbed down from the truck in Czechoslovakia, stiff and overheated, our throats dry as straw. There we boarded a train for Germany. Just as we were settling into our seats and thinking the worst was behind us, the conductor asked for identification. When he discovered that we had none, he threw us off. We waited until nightfall, then crossed the border by foot and made our way through Vienna and into Munich. We traveled by night, a haunting reminder of my years in hiding. This time, however, I had Joe with me for love and protection. And that made all the difference.

In Munich, we went straight to the Jewish council for assistance. They assigned Joe and me an apartment that belonged to a Nazi family, telling us to evict the owners. We knew what it was to be thrown out of a house, however, and so we took just one room and let them have the rest. The son had been wounded in the war and had very little use of his right hand. Whenever he passed us, he said, "*Heil* Hitler." That was not so pleasant, but the mother was very kind. She used to buy fish and cook it for us.

One day, my childhood friend Chajka Schiffman came to visit. Her cheeks were hollow and unnaturally pale, but she was still beautiful. The only two of our group who had survived, we held each other for a long time, aching, I think, as much for what we had as for what we had lost. She dropped onto the sofa next to me, coughing and chain-smoking, saying that she needed money. Her husband was a monster, she said, but her young daughter was enough to keep her getting up every morning. I gave her what I had and poured out my soul to her. When she left, we promised to keep in touch. Watching her go felt like losing my family all over again, but she had a family of her own to return to. I heard that she died a few years later in eastern Europe, broken and impoverished.

# Leo
## *Postscript*

So crowded, the train from Kraków to Munich! And, with all those people, to feel so alone! Fay and Joe and I, you couldn't pull us apart in Kraków. And now this. To split us up was the right thing, but to be all by myself again, even for a little while, was so hard for me. I was young. Only twenty-two. Just a small person in the middle of such a grand adventure. Though I'd had more than enough adventure already. What I would have given just to live quiet and safe again! I had to keep reminding myself that I was on this train in order to achieve that kind of life.

All the time on the train the conductor was checking papers. I didn't have papers, but that was on purpose. I would have had to go back to Kanczuga to get documentation for those papers, and set foot in that town again I would never do. In Munich, I could get papers for America through the Joint Distribution Committee. That was my plan.

So, without papers, I was always moving from one wagon to the next, heading for whichever one the conductor had just left. The ride to Munich took six, maybe seven hours. If I wasn't changing my seat, I was keeping my head down. Sleeping with my eyes open. Looking up only to nibble a bit of sandwich or sip a little water.

Munich was a misery, a bombed-out city, every second house a pile of rubble, the same condition as the refugees and the soldiers who filled its streets like a spreading mold. Young men with crutches, bandages on their brows, missing a leg or an arm. Yet, life went on, people took buses, did a little this and that, made a life for themselves.

Right away I started up again with the black market, because I didn't expect to stay long enough to find a trade. Even if you had a trade, there wasn't anywhere to work, because most of the places of business were gone. But, if there had been work, the Germans probably would have been happy to hire a Jew. They were afraid to show anti-Semitism, especially those who were guilty of crimes against the Jews. They were worried about criminal charges. Things were worse in Poland. Even after the war, the Poles were not afraid of us. The majority, they were happy there were no more Jews. They got our homes. They believed their poverty was the fault of the Jews. But the Germans, after the war, they had to learn how to adjust to a new life. Those who didn't like Hitler felt guilty; maybe they should have done something. Those who had been for Hitler, they had to watch out.

The refugees who came to Munich were always on the lookout for people they might have known before the war. I knew my family wasn't alive, but maybe somewhere there were cousins. Every time a new person came in, someone said, "Where are you from?" This was the daily routine.

I met up again with my sister and brother-in-law in a community center housed in one of the few buildings still standing. Most of the survivors went there. It had several large rooms and offices. I didn't meet anybody else from before. But the Jews, we were like a family. You stayed together, you talked together, telling your life stories, discussing what you were going to do. There were dozens and dozens of people, maybe a hundred. We sat at tables and chairs, drinking tea or coffee from little white cups. I began to feel very warm toward these people, and I made a few good friends.

The tone was serious, but not like at a funeral. The ones who had it the worst were those who hoped their families were alive. They were tense and anxious. This I have learned: uncertainty is worst. Wondering about younger people gone to Siberia. Wondering about those who had disappeared. At least Fay and I knew that this was it. When my parents and my little sisters left me in that barn, I knew it was the last time I'd ever see them. Somehow, you have that feeling. Only my older sister did I hope to find again.

Still, we had many relatives. "Nu," I asked everyone I met. "Did you hear from the Rosenbluths?"

Sometimes I was thrilled to hear, "So-and-so told me they saw . . ." But that was rare.

On the walls of the community center were lists of names from different towns, a few individual signs saying *I am looking for* . . . At the same time, people were interested in starting fresh. We were most of us in our twenties; young people were the only ones strong enough to survive. A young man would find a young lady he liked and ask for a date. Most of us, especially those who had lost their loves, were looking for a home life, for a person we could love. I went out with a few girls once or twice, but nothing serious.

Faiga and Joe went to the community center with me. Her hearing wasn't too good, but she was so terrific at reading lips that almost nobody could tell. People were speaking Polish, since a big percentage were from Poland. A lot of Polish Jews spoke Polish to each other; they grew up speaking it in their homes. Only very Orthodox families like ours spoke Yiddish. But Yiddish was the international language at the center. People from Czechoslovakia, Hungary, they all spoke Yiddish, because they didn't know each other's language.

In Munich, I got papers; then Faiga and Joe and I went from Munich to Bremenhaven. I got on a boat a month before they did. When they went to the pier to say goodbye, it was like a national holiday. Maybe a thousand Jews and other refugees were crowding the decks, waving and carrying on.

My sister held me so tightly I was thinking she would break the skin. "Have a good trip!" she said. "*Dowidzenia!* See you soon!"

The Ernie Pyle was a military transport. Thirteen days we sat on that boat, in the middle of February, with storms in the middle of the night, and the boat shaking so bad that nobody was eating. Except for me, I should say. I must've had fifty frankfurters, because I'd never tasted anything like them before. They put me in mind of kielbasa, but they were even better. I sat around with my new friends Robert Tessler and Julius Reiner, joking and reading, telling stories, playing cards and dominoes, reading newspapers. We even tried to learn a little English. By the time we landed, I knew the words "thank you," "hello," and "goodbye." Not exactly a Yankee yet, but I was on my way.

When I stepped off the ship in New York Harbor, all I could think was how beautiful it was. The silver skyscrapers on the horizon looked like nothing I'd ever seen. Even better, I was thrilled to find a relative waiting for me at the dock. Rabbi Gardenhaus was a distant cousin on my mother's side, an old man with a long, white beard. He helped me finish up my immigration paperwork and took me to his house in Brooklyn. He had plans for me, Rabbi Gardenhaus did. He wanted me to go to the yeshiva, study Jewish law. On my first day in America, he took me to a barber. I had beautiful long hair, but he told the barber in English to cut off all my hair so that I could wear a shtreimel, the big black hat my father had worn.

219

I said to the barber in Yiddish, "What are you going to do with my hair?" When he told me, I said, "Don't do it! You can trim it, that's all."

To my uncle I said, "I will catch a cold if you cut off all my hair!"

I held my breath, waiting for his anger. His son was a rabbi; his whole family was Orthodox. He was my only family in all of America. But I had been through too much to be kidding either him or myself.

To my surprise, he let me get the haircut I wanted. But, back on the street, he told me how disappointed he was.

I swallowed hard. "There are things to do in a rush way and things to do in a slow way," I said at last. "I'm not going to become a Hasid overnight. I'm not used to it anymore. When I was home as a child, it was fine, but many years have passed since then. My outlook on life is a little different now."

My imposing-looking uncle sighed and wrapped a heavy arm around my shoulders. "I'm not going to pressure you," he said. "When you're ready, you'll tell me."

Right away, I loved him. But I was tortured to be in his house, living that Orthodox life that no longer had any meaning for me. I stayed with him until my sister came. Then I said we had to get an apartment.

Not long after, the Hebrew Immigrant Aid Society got me a job as a shipping clerk in a cutlery distribution center in Manhattan. Every day I rode the subway from Brooklyn. At night I went to Thomas Jefferson High School. The classes were in English, but I worked hard, and somehow I managed to graduate.

I wanted a better job, but it was hard for me because of the language. Then, one day, I met an older man in Lynbrook, Long Island, who spoke Yiddish. He did glasswork and paid me forty dollars a week to start. Soon I went from glass to mirrors, working back in Brooklyn for a small mirror manufacturer. The guy was deaf, but because of Andzia and my sister, I knew how to communicate with him. He was very disorganized. His shop was such a mess that he could never find anything and could hardly make a living. It reminded me of my father's lesson in leather-cutting long ago: Never cut a piece when a smaller one already exists. Get as much from one piece as you can. I saw potential in that field, but not the way he was running it.

One day he came into the shop, and he almost had a heart attack. Where was all the merchandise? The whole place looked empty, because I had arranged everything in proper position according to size.

My boss had a customer, the Bulova watch company, that made up maybe eighty percent of his business. One day Bulova decided not to use him anymore. Just like that. My boss sat in a corner of his shop and started to cry.

Right away I went to the president of the company and told him that my boss barely made a living and that he depended on his business.

"It's very unfair," I said. I looked around that big, fancy office as if I had suddenly been dropped onto another planet. "You as a human being can't do that to another human being. You can't just cut him out."

It wasn't until I stopped speaking that I realized I couldn't stop my right leg from shaking. I wondered whether my English had come out okay. Then I wondered where I'd gotten such chutzpah.

The president was a man not much younger than my boss. When he stood up from behind that big desk, I cowered a little.

"You know," he said, rubbing his chin. "You have touched me very much. This will not happen. We will give him back the account."

It may seem unbelievable that I could have done such a thing. Me, just off the boat and not even knowing English so well. But when you live through tragedies, common sense becomes the most important thing. This is the way I have run my life. Whichever way you wind up in a situation, go for common sense.

I stayed with that old man for a while, but it was not a pleasant place to work. He hated his wife; she was always bothering him. And he had very little to pay me. I started to think about my future. I realized that if I went door-to-door to big customers, they could give me as much business as twenty people, and with fewer headaches. So I left him and started out on my own.

There were a lot of survivors and refugees around at that time, and every weekend we went into New York City for dances and socializing. We had a lot of fun. One Saturday night in the early 1950s, a woman who knew me met a young girl named Ethel Biglaiser at a family party. Ethel was lovely, very intelligent, a hard worker from a very fine American home. The woman was a friend of Ethel's aunt. She asked the aunt whether Ethel was seeing anybody, because she knew a nice fellow she thought Ethel should meet.

The aunt gave her Ethel's number, she gave it to me, and I called. Ethel said she was sorry, but she was busy.

I said, "I'm going to call you one more time. If you don't have time then, I won't call you anymore."

Again such chutzpah! She was so annoyed, that greenhorn dictating

221

to her! But I'd made her curious. So the next time I called, she agreed to go out.

It was love at first sight for me. We got married six months later, in the biggest snowstorm in history, it must have been. The trains stopped running, the maid of honor got stuck somewhere near Philadelphia, the musicians had to walk half the way. Ethel's father, who had the keys to the liquor cabinet in the wedding hall, was late because he had to walk from the East to the West Bronx. So, most of the time, nobody could even have a drink. Ethel was in tears. Only about half of the two hundred guests could get there, but my sister and Joe were there, which was all I cared about. My family, as little as it was, was represented. My parents, may they rest in peace, would have *kvelled* with pride.

My new life grew, with the births of three beautiful sons and a healthy business in Queens. Still I could not forget the past. To Andzia, who had cared for me back in Poland, I sent hundreds of dollars and packages of clothing. She wrote to us, "I put the clothes on the bed and started to cry. Never would I have believed there were such beautiful things in the world." When my youngest son had his bar mitzvah, we sent Andzia a ticket. I picked her up from the airport, and right away I recognized her, even from a distance. She was older, of course, but that smile I'd know anywhere.

Today I have six grandchildren and homes in New Jersey and Florida, and I consider myself a very lucky person. I have lived a long life and have shared it with my wonderful family. Over the years, I have come to see the glass as half-full rather than half-empty. The way I see it, I was in the wrong place in the wrong time, and I lived through a terrible tragedy. But I have lived. Things happen, terrible things. It's a part of life. You have to accept and be grateful for what you have.

I used to think more about the old days than I do now. Every time I met my friends from Kanczuga, we'd sit for hours and talk about the shtetl, about this person and that person. We'd talk about that time as if it had been a paradise, but it was no paradise. Still, we had our families, our friends, and those days won't come back. Those days you're always going to cherish. But we also have to cherish the things we have now.

Today, I am happy. I am happy that my children are happy. Tragedies happen. Somebody kills part of your family, you can't say that your life is finished. You have to go on with your life.

When I left my parents to go into hiding, my mother told me to stay alive so that the family name should not disappear. All the time I hid, my purpose was to keep the name alive. But later, I realized there's more to it than a name. There's a family tree. There are the future generations. We should do something with our lives. We should contribute more to humanity than just a name.

# Fay
## *Postscript*

After all our traveling, we were not much closer to America. The Hebrew Immigrant Aid Society finally gave us passports and visas, but they did not know when we would be able to leave. As always, we hoped for the best. In anticipation of our new life, Joe and I bought some paintings from a street vendor, one with colorful flowers in a vase, the other of a mama cat and her kittens. Joe also bought me a little gold brooch in the shape of a bowtie. Anyone might have taken us for just another young married couple, full of expectations for a happy future.

We were told we would be leaving from Bremenhaven, a lovely port city of monuments and fine, well-kept boulevards. For several months, we lived in army barracks there, waiting for word. One long, empty day stretched into another. We walked around the city, talking about the future and doing our best to forget the past. Just when we thought we could stand no more waiting, a dockworkers' strike broke out in New York, which held us up even longer. We were running out of money, so we sold a few things to buy food.

One day, Joe and I were walking down the street when a policeman stopped us. He asked Joe for identification. My husband, who had lived in Germany before the war, was in no mood to be polite.

"Why should I show you identification, you Nazi?" he asked.

The policeman immediately put him under arrest. I had to think fast. If he arrested me, too, no one would know what had happened to us. So I jumped on a passing tram before the man knew what was happening. I was still shaking when I reached the barracks. One of the American officers spoke Polish, and he agreed to help me. He took me to the jail, where I found Joe on a little stool in a cell. His mouth was a tight line of fury.

"Don't worry," I said. "We'll get you out somehow."

Always a man of few words, my husband sighed and turned away.

The American officer asked his superiors for a lawyer. When the lawyer contacted the German police, he was told that they would not free Joe without a trial.

"After all," the lawyer said apologetically, "your husband was very rude."

I brushed this off. "When will they hold the trial?"

He shrugged. "They told me they will make it as soon as possible."

That night, I lay alone in the barracks, wondering what I would do if the word came for us to go to America and Joe was still in jail. At some point before dawn, I fell onto my knees in anguish. Oh God, I prayed. What more do you want from me? When will you have your fill of my pain?

God didn't answer. But when dawn broke, I knew what I had to do. I could not leave Europe without my husband. I would simply have to stay.

Early the next morning, the lawyer appeared at the door. "Get dressed quickly," he said. "The trial is set for nine o'clock!"

We ate a hurried breakfast together at the mess tent. The lawyer was so kind that I felt my spirits lift despite my misgivings.

By the time the trial began, however, I could no longer hold back my tears. I glanced over at Joe, who sat stolidly, staring into space.

The judge took pity on us. He said, "I'll let you go, Herr Walker, but I must remind you in the future to be respectful to the police. They are here to protect you."

A week later, the strike was lifted, and we sailed for New York City.

The Hebrew Immigrant Aid Society put up Luzer, Joe, and me in a little hotel on the west side of Manhattan, but we didn't plan to stay there long. Joe soon found a distant cousin who helped us get settled. We rented an apartment in Brooklyn. A friend of Joe's from Berlin gave him a job as an egg candler, which meant he checked eggs for signs of fertilization to determine whether they were kosher. His salary was sixty-five dollars a week. When a friend asked him what his wife did with all that money, he said, "She counts it!"

We had enough to live comfortably, but I had no intention of sitting home all day. A friend took me to an employment agency, where I found a job with a Jewish boss cutting fabric for a lingerie factory. From there, I progressed to making skirts and blouses, then eventually graduated to expensive dresses. Once again, Mamche's training served me well.

During this time, I took an American name: Fay. Far from feeling the

225

desperation that made me become Fela, I was proud to be in America and wanted to fit in. Luzer did the same, changing his name to Leo.

Joe and I moved to Florida in 1977. To my sorrow, we were never able to have children. My doctors do not know why. Perhaps the injury to my head that eventually robbed me of my hearing affected my central nervous system, as well. Perhaps the years under constant stress and without proper nourishment took their toll. I only know that the Nazis robbed me both of the generations that came before and those that would have come after me.

Nevertheless, my life in America has not been without pleasure. My dear husband, who died in 1996, was my chauffeur, telephone operator, and constant source of love and support. I have had many precious friends and family members, both survivors and those who were spared the horror of war. I traveled to Israel ten times and support it with my prayers and contributions.

On one of those visits, I met a man, a cousin of Joe's, and we fell deeply in love. My husband knew; the whole family knew. I seriously considered marrying the man, but, in the end, I could not bear the scandal. To this day, I wonder how my life would have been different had I married one of the men for whom I had felt such passion. But God has his reasons for keeping people apart.

On my most recent birthday, I was eighty-two years old. If my survival has had a purpose, it is to deliver this testimony. It is a debt I owe not only to the millions who perished in concentration camps, died from starvation, and were shot down in their homes, but also to those who wish only to live in peace.

Of the two brothers I met outside the watchman's hut, one was murdered in Kanczuga after liberation; the other married and moved to Australia.

Of our Rabbi Westreich's eight children, only one survived.

My cousins Halina and Pnina Rosenbluth survived in Siberia and now live in Israel.

Arie and Piniu were the only two members of Bruchcia Laufer's family to survive. Arie went to Israel before the war; Piniu was sent to Siberia and then emigrated to America.

Many wonderful people in the Polish villages helped my brother, myself, and others like us live through the years in hiding. But, today, few people in my hometown acknowledge that Jews once lived and died there. Throughout the world, many still doubt that the Holocaust occurred at all. I have told my story to counter these claims and to honor the memories of my family and friends:

Our parents, Balci and Itczy Rosenbluth, and our sisters, Tunia and Senia.

Our uncle Sruly Rosenbluth and his family.

Our uncle David Rosenbluth and his family.

Our father's cousin Yossi Kneller and his family.

My friends Bruchcia, Runia, Genendla, Faiga, Malka, Gittel, and Chajka, and their families.

Mayer Langsam.

My loved ones, I assure you that I have not forgotten you. You have been with me all these years, day and night. In my mind, you will always be young. You would not recognize me. I am old and sick. But I have survived for a purpose: to make sure that your memory lives on.

I am alone; you are together for all time. No one is there to say kaddish for you. No one is left. Only my brother, Luzer, and I, who will always be your Faiga.

We cannot visit you, my beloveds, because our Kanczuga is a murderous town, and we have vowed never to return. But we hold you forever in our hearts.